AMiguRuMi KniTs

patterns for 20 cute mini knits

Creative Publishing international

HaNsi SiNgH

**Creative Publishing
international**

First published in the United States of America by
Creative Publishing International, Inc., a member of
Quayside Publishing Group
400 First Avenue North
Suite 300
Minneapolis, MN 55401
1-800-328-3895
www.creativepub.com

ISBN-13: 978-1-58923-435-2
ISBN-10: 1-58923-435-9
10 9 8 7 6 5 4 3 2 1

Library of Congress Cataloging-in-Publication Data
Singh, Hansi.
  Amigurumi knits : patterns for 20 cute mini knits / Hansi Singh.
     p. cm.
  Includes index.
  ISBN-13: 978-1-58923-435-2
  ISBN-10: 1-58923-435-9
  1. Knitting--Patterns. I. Title.

  TT825.S548 2009
  746.43'2041--dc22
                            2008049232

Cover & Book Design: everlution design
Page Layout: everlution design
Photographs: Glenn Scott Photography, project step-out photographs by Hansi Singh
Technical Editor: Rita Greenfeder
Copy Editor: Lucia Raatma
Proofreader: India Tresselt

Printed in Singapore

What is Amigurumi?

Amigurumi isn't a word that you can find in *Webster's Abridged*. Not yet. But with its meteoric rise to popularity, it's only a matter of time before it sneaks its way into everyday parlance.

Originally derived from the Japanese, the word literally means "encompassing knit." In recent years, it's come to include crocheted, as well as knitted, plush creations that are defined by one little word: cute. Sometimes overbearingly killer creepy cute, but cute, nonetheless.

Though amigurumi has become the obsession of choice for the crochet community in recent years, the knitting community has been a little slower on the uptake. Even now, it's difficult to find patterns for knitted amigurumi.

In a small way, I hope that this book can carve its way into the heart of the knitting world, introducing the idea of knitted amigurumi to the fiber artists of the globe. There's no reason why knitters can't enjoy creating amigurumi critters. We can't let the crocheters keep all the cuteness to themselves, can we?

When most people think of knitting, they think of scarves, socks, and sweaters; mittens, perhaps; maybe a wrist cuff or a headband. But squishy stuffed things? Why would anyone want to knit those? Well, for those who doubt, naysay, or wag their heads at this obsession, here are ten marvelous reasons why knitting amigurumi really IS the best pastime out there—period.

A Top 10 List:
Why you will love Knitting amigurumi

1. It takes much less time than knitting a sweater.

I don't know about you, but I like projects that have a definite beginning, middle, and end. Sweaters have a beginning (you have to cast-on somewhere, don't you?) and then a middle—a very long, tedious, endless middle, if you're as impatient and easily distracted as I am. Squishies, on the other hand, always have an end in sight. If you have difficulty seeing a project from start to finish, knitting amigurumi is the thing for you. Most of the time, you can muster the gumption to finish up your critter.

2. It takes much less yarn than a sweater.

The only thing more daunting to me than the amount of time that it takes to knit a sweater is the amount of yarn. Most sweaters require more than 1,000 yards (914 m) of yarn. I could never commit to that, no matter how lush and scrumptious the yarn is. Squishies, on the other hand, require a much smaller yarn commitment. For most projects, about 100 to 200 yards (91 to 184 m) will do. Thank goodness for that!

3. It won't keep you warm!

Some of us live in places where keeping ourselves warm is a high priority. I live in Seattle, for example, and the winters are blustering enough that I always try to squeeze a couple of hat and mitten projects into my knitting queue in the early fall. But that leaves about eight months of the year when I don't want to be knitting countless pairs of wrist warmers or scarflettes. It's during this time that I appreciate knitting squishies. If I lived in Fiji, I would sit on the beach year-round and solely (with a perpetual smile) knit amigurumi.

4. It helps you become a precise, highly adept knitter.

When you're working on a sweater or a scarf, you'll often find something like this in the pattern instructions: "CO 100 sts and work straight for 20" (51 cm)." When you're knitting squishies, on the other hand, such loose instruction is nearly nonexistent. Nearly every nanometer of your project will contain some sort of increase, decrease, short row, or combination of maneuvers. In addition to keeping your attention engaged, the variety of techniques that you'll constantly be using in your project will make a knitting technician out of you, requiring you to hone your existing skills and to learn many more. Plus, the skills that you pick up by knitting amigurumi will transfer to nearly any other sort of knitting you decide to try.

5. It makes you popular among your friends.

As soon as you begin knitting squishies, the eyes of people around you will light up with the fire of interest. Not to accuse people of opportunism, but nearly everyone will want a piece of the action. People you barely know will mention their upcoming birthdays as they gush over the amigurumi octopus sitting on your mantle. When people start laying claim to all the beautiful creatures flying from your needles, just smile and nod, vaguely staring off into the distance. Over time, they'll come to realize that the only way to get in on the action is to take up knitting themselves. Then, brace yourself for innumerable requests for knitting lessons!

6. It makes you popular among the small children in your life.

Once you begin knitting amigurumi, you will become Santa Claus to every child you know (even without the red and white suit, fake belly, and snow-white beard). As soon as they see you, the kids will flock about you, demanding to see the latest squishy project you've completed. Soon, as your critter passes from one little hand to the next amid oohs and aahs, you'll hear the requests. "I want one!" And when you do begin handing out squishy snails and squids at birthdays and baby showers, you'll have the high honor of being just about the coolest adult around.

7. It keeps your hands busy.

I began knitting when I was seven months pregnant. I honestly believe that the desire to knit was in some way linked to that notorious nesting instinct that afflicts pregnant women in the latter stage of their pregnancy. I had an irresistible urge to do something, anything, with my hands. The usual ways that I occupied myself, including writing, sketching, and dancing, just didn't seem to cut it. And so, I took up knitting. Now, two years later (and counting), that obsessive desire to do something with my hands has transformed itself into something life-changing. But no matter how many amigurumi pieces I complete or patterns I design, the act of knitting remains the same, worked one stitch at a time. The same tactility implicit in needles and yarn that kept me occupied while I was waiting for the birth of my son continues to sustain me in my creative life. Whatever your passion, the meditative act of needles clicking and yarn passing through your fingers is sure to inspire you.

8. It helps you decorate your surroundings with lovely handmade things.

Who doesn't want a jellyfish hanging from their car's rearview mirror, or a fierce black-devil anglerfish dangling its lure on their mantle? Once you begin knitting amigurumi, you're home, office space, or car will be bare no longer. If you start having to hide your amigurumi critters in boxes in the garage, however, just remember one thing: ceiling hooks are great.

9. It helps clean out your yarn stash.

Often when I buy yarn, I don't buy it with a specific project in mind, but rather because it looks utterly divine and irresistible, curled up and delicious within its comfortable skein. I almost never think of what I could do with it other than brushing it against my cheek and pondering its squishy cuddliness. As you can imagine, this type of impulse yarn purchasing has led to accumulating quite a fiber stash. But by knitting amigurumi, I've figured out that I can, in fact, work my way through my stash one skein at a time. Amigurumi projects are wonderful, quick stash-busters. Most require one skein or less of yarn. You can make brilliant ultramarine angora-merino blend slugs, a heathered navy qiviut Nessie, or any other quirky critter that your heart yearns for. If only stashes weren't so easy to replenish...

10. It provides countless hours of addictive pleasure.

Most people who knit squishies find the process very addictive. The most fascinating part of the process seems to be the way that your little flat piece of knitting acquires a life of its very own. It suddenly transforms from just another yarn-thing to a recognizable little creature. The evolution is nearly magical. With every critter that I make, the transformation never fails to surprise me.

How to Use this Book

This book is divided into two main sections. The first section consists of detailed explanations, combined with photographic illustrations, of the salient techniques you'll need for knitting amigurumi. The second section is chock-full of knit amigurumi projects. If you're a fairly new knitter, my recommendation is to go through the techniques section first. If there's a technique that you're unfamiliar with, be sure to cast on and try it before diving into a project that requires it. If, on the other hand, you're an experienced knitter, you can probably pick a project that piques your interest and get started. If it happens to contain a few techniques that you haven't tried before, you can always refer to the appropriate how-to section for guidance along the way.

And whether you're a novice knitter or an expert knitter, always remember to have fun! Happy amigurumi knitting!

Techniques

The Basics

•••

These are the techniques that you need to knit, no matter what you knit. In this book, I assume that you've already made your first simple items: a scarf, a washcloth, a simple hat, or other things along that vein. So, you probably already know how to do the long-tail cast-on, knit a stitch, purl a stitch, and the basic bind-off. In this section, I'll give you a quick overview of these techniques, and introduce some new concepts relating to casting on, knitting, purling, and binding off that will help you in your amigurumi knitting adventures!

Casting-on

These are the methods for getting stitches on your needle. The standard is the long-tail cast-on, which is the default way to get stitches on your needle if the pattern doesn't specify another method.

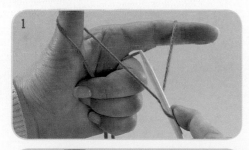

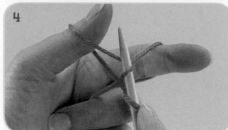

Long-tail cast-on

Long-tail Cast-on

Make a slipknot on the needle and hold the needle in your right hand. Put the thumb and index finger of your left hand between the tail and working yarn, the tail around your thumb and the working yarn around your index finger. Use the other fingers of your left hand to hold both strands snugly against your left palm (1). Insert the needle upward through the loop on your thumb (2). Pivot the needle to the right and go over and under the yarn on your index finger, picking up a loop (3). Pull the loop back down through the thumb loop (4). Let your thumb drop out of the loop. Spread your fingers to snug up the new stitch on the needle (5). Repeat the steps for each stitch.

Cable Cast-on

There are a couple more cast-on methods that are particularly useful for amigurumi knitting. The first is the cable cast-on method. This is particularly useful if you need to add an extended line of stitches to your knitting after you've already worked several rows or rounds. Insert the right needle into the space between the last two stitches on your left needle. Throw the yarn around your needle from this position (1) and pull a loop through. Put this loop back on your left needle (2). You've just cast on one stitch. Continue in this manner, adding as many stitches as the pattern calls for (3).

Cable cast-on

(continued)

Knit Cast-on

Another useful cast-on for amigurumi knitting is the knit-on method. It creates an extremely tight, inelastic edge, which is especially useful in certain circumstances, such as when you are working the inner corkscrew of a shell. Create a slipknot, and place it on your needle to create your first loop. Now, insert your needle into the loop knitwise. Wrap your yarn around your needle (1) and pull a loop through. Place this loop on your left needle (2). You have just cast on one stitch. Continue in this manner until you have cast on the required number of stitches (3). Notice that the knit-on cast on is very similar to the cable cast-on. The difference lies in where you insert your needle. This slight difference makes all the difference in the world in the resulting cast-on edge!

Knit cast-on

Knit the standard way

Knitting, Purling, and Working Through Back Loops (K-tbl and P-tbl)

To knit the standard way, insert your right needle through the last loop on your left needle from left to right, wrap the yarn around your right needle (1), and pull a loop through, simultaneously dropping the stitch off of your left needle (2). But, what if you insert your right needle through the last loop on your left needle from right to left (3)? When you do this, you are knitting the stitch through the back loop (abbreviated K-tbl). The resulting stitch looks like a knit stitch but is tight and twisted (4).

Knit through back loop

To purl the standard way, bring your yarn to the front of the work, insert your needle from right to left through the last loop on your left needle, wrap the yarn around the needle (1), and pull a loop through onto your right needle while dropping the old loop off your left needle (2). To create a stitch that is twisted from the purl side, purl the stitch through the back loop (abbreviated P-tbl). Insert your needle from left to right through the last loop of your left needle (3) and continue to make a purl stitch in the same way (4).

1

2

Purl the standard way

3

4

Purl through back loop

Simple Stitch Patterns

The most commonly used stitch patterns in knitting amigurumi include stockinette stitch, reverse stockinette stitch, and garter stitch. Each of them has different characteristics that make them appropriate for different knitting situations.

In stockinette stitch, the fabric, consists of calm V-shaped stitches. In addition to being neat and unobtrusive, stockinette stitch is an ideal medium for executing the many shaping maneuvers used for amigurumi. When knit in rows, stockinette stitch consists of all knit stitches on the right side, and all purl stitches on the wrong side. When knit in the round, you simply knit all stitches.

Stockinette

Reverse stockinette stitch is nearly identical to stockinette. In fact, it is merely the wrong side of the stockinette stitch pattern. Instead of knitting all right side rows, you purl them, and instead of purling all wrong side rows, you knit them. Instead of the neat V-shaped stitches that characterize stockinette stitch, you'll see a series of interlock I stitches. While stockinette stitch is smooth, reverse stockinette stitch is bumpy, giving it a pebbly, mottled feel.

Reverse stockinette

The final frequently used stitch in amigurumi is garter stitch. Garter stitch is, possibly, the easiest stitch pattern in all of knitting. To work garter stitch flat, you simply knit all right and wrong side rows. To work garter stitch in the round, you alternate knit and purl rounds. Unlike stockinette and reverse stockinette stitch, which produce tight fabrics that curl, garter stitch produces a springy fabric that always lies flat. Like reverse stockinette stitch, the bumpy purl stitches are prominent, and garter stitch has lots of texture.

Garter stitch

Slip and Slide
(Sl1 knitwise and Sl1 purlwise)

Slipping a stitch is easy. You just move your stitch from the left needle to right needle without doing anything to it. But, there are some important subtleties even in this simple action. When you slip a stitch by inserting your right needle from right to left into the other stitch (the same way you would if you were going to purl that stitch), you are slipping a stitch purlwise. If, on the other hand, you slip a stitch by inserting your needle through it from left to right (the way you would if you were going to knit that stitch), you are slipping the stitch knitwise. In amigurumi knitting, you'll mainly be slipping the first stitch of every row knitwise. This helps create a selvedge that is relatively easy to pick up stitches from, and is great for seaming.

Sl1 purlwise

Sl1 knitwise

Binding Off (BO)

Most knitters are familiar with the conventional bind-off method, where you knit a stitch, and, using your left needle, lift the second stitch on the right needle up and over the stitch that you've just knit. In general, this is the default method for binding off stitches. When a pattern just tells you to bind off all stitches, this is the method to use.

In addition to this default method, there are many other ways to bind off stitches. Most are simple variations on the default bind-off method, involving a combination of knitting or purling as you bind off.

Purl Two Together Bind-Off

For this common method of binding off, purl two stitches together (1), transfer this stitch back to your left needle (2), and purl two stitches again (3). Repeat this operation until you've bound off the required number of stitches.

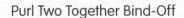

P2tog bind-off

Three-Needle Bind-Off

One crucial method for binding off in amigurumi knitting is the three-needle bind off. This method allows you to bind off two edges simultaneously and, amazingly, join these edges together. As you can imagine, using this method can really save a lot of time that otherwise would have been spent binding off each of the edges separately and seaming them together.

Hold the two pieces that you're joining with their right sides facing each other*. Then, insert your needle knitwise through the first stitch on the front needle and through the first stitch on the back needle (1). Wrap the yarn around the tip of your needle, and pull a loop through both stitches as you simultaneously drop the stitches from the front and back needles (2). Repeat these steps to get a second stitch onto your right needle.

* Binding off with right sides together creates an invisible seam. To create a decorative ridge, bind off with wrong sides together.

Once you have two stitches on your right needle, use the tip of the left needle to lift the second stitch on your right needle up and over the first stitch (3), thus binding off one stitch. Continue in this way, and you'll have all stitches bound off, and your two pieces will be attached.

Three-needle bind off

Shaping

Amigurumi creatures, like their real-life or imaginary counterparts, are characterized by their unique shapes. Fortunately, as knitters, we have many tricks up our sleeves for shaping: decreasing the number of stitches on the needle, increasing the number of stitches on the needle, and adding short rows into the work. The quick and dirty recipe for shaping knitting goes like this: Adding another row increases the length of the shape.

Increasing or decreasing the number of stitches in the row increases or decreases the width of the shape. Adding short rows causes portions of the shape to protrude forward or backward in space. When you put these three techniques together, you are able to adjust your knitting in all three dimensions! And, you can knit just about any three-dimensional object you want to—awesome!

Decreasing

Here are various ways to decrease the number of stitches. Each method provides a distinct appearance.

Two Stitches to One (K2tog and SSK)

One way to decrease the number of stitches on the needle is to combine two stitches together. The simplest way to do this is to knit two stitches together, abbreviated K2tog. Knitting two stitches together has a definite orientation: it is right-leaning. This means that whenever you knit two stitches together, the stitch on the left always leans to the right and sits on top of the stitch on the right. Insert needle knitwise into two stitches together, wrap the yarn around the needle (1), pull the loop through (2).

Knit two together (K2tog)

To create a left-leaning decrease that mirrors knitting two stitches together, slip-slip-knit (abbreviated SSK). Slip the two stitches knit-wise, one at a time (1), and insert your left needle into them to knit them together (2). You have decreased one stitch and the right stitch leans on top of the left stitch.

Slip-slip-knit (SSK)

(continued)

Two Stitches to One on the Purl Side (P2tog and P2tog-tbl)

What if you need to decrease while you're working on the wrong side of the fabric? This is when purling two stitches together (abbreviated P2tog) and purling two stitches together through their back loops (abbreviated P2tog-tbl) come into the game.

To create a right-leaning decrease from the wrong side of the work, purl two stitches together: insert the right needle into two stitches purlwise, wrap yarn around tip of right needle (1), and pull a loop through (2).

Purl two together (P2tog)

To create a left-leaning decrease from the wrong side of the work, on the other hand, we have to purl two stitches together through their back loops. This is definitely one of the most awkward moves in all of knitting! Turning the work slightly to see the backside, insert the right needle left to right through the two end stitches. Then, wrap the yarn around the tip of your right needle (1), and, with as few expletives as possible, pull a loop through onto your right needle (2).

Purl two together through back loop (P2tog-tbl)

Three Stitches to One (Sl2-K1-P2SSO and Sl2-P1-P2SSO)

It's also useful to be able to turn three stitches into one stitch. Though there are many ways to do this, my favorite method by far is the central stitch double decrease, abbreviated Sl2-K1-P2SSO. Unlike other three-to-one decreases, this decrease doesn't have a slant to it. Instead, the central stitch remains on top, creating a neat, symmetrical appearance, an effect that satisfies the neat freak in me.

To work the decrease from the right side of the work, slip two stitches together by inserting your needle knitwise into both simultaneously (1), knit the next stitch, and, using the tip of the left needle, lift the two slipped stitches up and over the stitch that you just knit (2) (3).

Central stitch double decrease (Sl2-K1-P2SSO)

Working this decrease from the wrong side of the work is similar. Abbreviated Sl2-P1-P2SSO, slip two stitches purlwise simultaneously through their back loops (1). Yes, this is an awkward move. Purl one stitch. Pass the slipped stitches simultaneously over the stitch just purled and off your needle (2).

If you turn your work over and look at the right side of the work, you'll discover an amazingly neat central stitch double decrease that's identical to the right side version (3).

Central stitch double decrease from the purl side (Sl2-P1-PSSO)

Increasing

Like most things in knitting, there are many ways to increase. Each of these different methods looks different, and is suitable for a different situation. All will prove to be useful in your amigurumi knitting adventures.

The Bar Increase (K-fb)

This is one of the simplest increases, and, unlike other modes of increasing, doesn't require you to learn a left and right version. It also doesn't boast of being invisible like other increasing methods. Instead, the new stitch that you create with this method will have a little bar at its base, which will be highly visible. Often, the bar increase, abbreviated K-fb, is used in situations where the bar blends in with the rest of the stitches (as in garter stitch) or when the bar serves a decorative function to highlight the line at which you are increasing stitches.

Knit a stitch, but don't drop it off your left needle (1). Now, insert your right needle into the back loop of the stitch (2), and knit it again, now allowing the stitch to slide off your left needle (3). Your single stitch will now have become two, with the second stitch branching from a little horizontal bar. One stitch increased. Yeah!

Bar increase (K-fb)

The Make-One Increases (M1R and M1L)

Make-one increases are nearly invisible, which makes this pair of increases an ideal choice in most amigurumi knitting situations.

To perform both the right and left versions of the make-one increase, you pick up the running yarn in between your needles, place it on your left needle, and knit into it. How you place the running yarn on your left needle and how you knit into the resulting loop varies, based on whether you are working the right or the left version of the increase.

Unlike decreases, which clearly have a direction in which they slant, increases have a slant that's much more subtle. Some expert knitters would argue that the visual differences between the left and right versions of the make-one increase are so slight that you don't really need to worry about learning two versions. This may be true when you are knitting a sweater. When you're knitting amigurumi, on the other hand, you're dealing with a sculpted palm-sized object, one in which the increase and decrease lines play a much more significant role in the way the work looks. In a small piece like this, small asymmetries in your increase lines will be easier to see than in a large piece like a sweater.

(continued)

So, it makes sense to use both right and left versions of the make-one increase, as this will make your right and left increase lines look more symmetrical, and make your amigurumi look more polished.

The right-leaning version of the make-one increase, abbreviated M1R, tends to be the default make-one increase to use. To work it, insert your right needle under the running yarn from front to back (1). Then, transfer the resulting loop onto your left needle (2). Now, knit into this loop in the normal way, thereby adding an extra stitch to your row (3).

Make-one right (M1R)

To work the left version of the make-one increase, abbreviated M1L, insert your *left* needle under the running yarn from front to back (1). transfer the loop to your left needle. Now, knit into the back loop of this stitch once again adding an extra stitch to your row.

Make-one left (M1L)

Note the subtle difference in the way these increases slant.

M1L, M1R in second row under needle

Lifting Up the Loop Increases (KRL and KLL)

Though the loop increases aren't nearly as neat as the make-one increases, they are useful in some situations. When you need to make many increases in one row, the running yarn can get extremely tight, and executing multiple make-one increases can be a challenge. The loop increases are also useful when you need to create two new stitches side by side.

And for those of us who have a hard time remembering a right and a left version of anything (a deficit I must confess to), the loop increases may be the only case in which the right and left versions are memorable. Seriously!

To work the loop increases, add an extra stitch by knitting into the head of the stitch in the row below the one you are working. As you might have guessed, you work the right version by knitting into the right side of this stitch, and you work the left version by knitting into the left side of the stitch.

To work the right version, abbreviated KRL, use your right needle to lift up the head of the stitch that's directly below the stitch on your left needle (1). Place this loop on your left needle (2) and knit into it (3), thereby adding an extra stitch to your row.

Right loop increase (KRL)

To work the left version of the loop increase, use your left needle to lift up the head of the stitch that's two stitches below the stitch on your right needle (1). Keep this loop on your left needle. Then knit into this loop (2), once again adding an extra stitch to your row.

Left loop increase (KLL)

The Yarn-Over Increase (YO)

If you're familiar with knitting lace or eyelets, you are probably already an expert. And you're probably wondering what an increase like this is doing in a book on amigurumi. After all, an amigurumi critter can't have holes if you expect it to hold in its stuffing! There are some places where the yarn-over increase is useful, particularly when you are creating parts for your critters that won't be stuffed.

The yarn-over increase, abbreviated YO, is one of the simplest increases to perform. Bring your yarn forward, wrap it, counterclockwise, around the right needle and return it to the back of the work (1). In the next row, knit or purl this wrap like any other stitch. The yarn-over increase leaves a hole (2).

Yarn over (YO)

The Magic of Short Rows

Increases and decreases can only adjust the width of a knitted shape. To also adjust its bulge, or the extent to which it protrudes forward or backward in space, we use short rows. Some knitters love short rows, while others shudder at their mere mention. After you've finished several of the projects in this book, you'll find that short rows are a simple, powerful technique for shaping your knitting.

How Do Short Rows Work?

A short row is exactly what it sounds like: a row that you add into your knitting that has fewer stitches than the number of stitches on your needle. Let's say, for example, that you have 20 stitches on your needle. Instead of knitting all 20, you knit only 10 of them, turn your knitting, and purl back to the beginning of your row. You've just added a short row into your knitting!

There are a couple of ways to add short rows into your knitting. If you add short rows to one side of your knitting, as we just discussed, you are making one selvedge of the work longer than the other selvedge.

Short rows on one side

(continued)

If you add short rows to the center of your knitting, on the other hand, you are making the central length of your work longer than the selvedge length. This will result in a central bump of stitches protruding forward (or backward) at the center of your work.

Short rows in the center

Wrapping and Turning (w&t)

Let's go back to that 10-stitch short row that you just added. If you worked the short row as described, you would find yourself with a big hole at the junction between the short row and the rest of your knitting. As it is, this opening would provide an ample opportunity for stuffing to escape from your finished toy. Not an attractive (or safe) possibility.

To avoid the holes that short rows can create in your knitting, perform an operation called wrapping and turning, abbreviated in knitter's lingo as w&t. Instead of knitting your short row and simply turning, knit your short row, wrap your yarn around the following unworked stitch, and only then turn and work back to the beginning of the row. How you wrap and turn depends on whether you are working on the knit side or the purl side of stockinette stitch fabric.

When working a short row on the knit side of the fabric, perform the wrap and turn operation as follows. Knit the required number of stitches, bring the yarn forward to the front of your work, slip the next (unworked) stitch from the left needle to the right needle **(1)**, bring the yarn to the back of your work, and slip the unworked stitch back to the left needle **(2)**. Now turn the knitting and purl the required number of stitches in the next row **(3)**.

Wrap and turn from knit side

When working a short row on the purl side of the fabric, you perform the wrap and turn slightly differently. After you have purled the required number of stitches and are ready to wrap the yarn around the next unworked stitch, the yarn will already be at the front of the work. To wrap the stitch, bring the yarn to the back of the work, slip the next unworked stitch from the left needle to the right needle **(1)**, bring the yarn to the front of the work again, and slip the unworked stitch back to the left needle **(2)**. Then, you're ready to turn and work the next row **(3)**.

Wrap and turn from purl side

Taking Care of Those Wraps

We've taken care of the holes, but there is another problem. When you wrap and turn, you are left with some unsightly little bars that highlight where you turned the short row. These bars are nearly invisible in garter stitch and reverse stockinette stitch, so when working in these patterns, you can simply knit past the wraps. However, the bars can be very unsightly in stockinette stitch and you must take care of these wraps of yarn in some way. The standard way is to knit or purl them when you pass them. Most patterns don't include notes on when you'll be passing these wraps. As a conscious knitter, you need to establish an awareness of when you're passing them and know how to take care of them.

When you pass a wrap on the purl side of the fabric (the wrong side in stockinette stitch), insert your right needle from front to back under the wrap (1) and place it onto your left needle, allowing it to sit on the right of the stitch around which it was wrapped (2). Then, purl the stitch and its wrap together (3). Though this will produce a bulbous yarn loop on the purl side of the fabric, you'll notice that the wrap will disappear from the knit side of the fabric, leaving an even, neat knit stitch (4).

Purling wrap with stitch

When you pass a wrap on the knit side of the fabric, first insert your right needle from front to back under the wrap (1). Then, lift the wrap onto your left needle, up and over the stitch that it was wrapped around (2). Slip first the stitch and then the wrap knitwise (3), and then knit them together (4). Note that this final step of slipping twice and knitting together is nearly identical to the slip-slip-knit (SSK) decrease.

Knitting wrap with stitch

Around and Around: Knitting in Circles

Lots of things are shaped like tubes: arms, fingers, legs, tentacles, toes, and horns, just to name a few. There are different ways to knit these tubes: to knit them flat and seam them, or to knit them in circles. Knitting in circles is known in knitter's parlance as knitting in the round. Knitting around and around is easy when you're working on something large, like the body of a sweater or an adult hat. You just find a circular needle that's large enough and cast on. If, on the other hand, you're trying to knit a tube that is too small to fit on a circular needle, you'll have to resort to other measures. And since most amigurumi tends to be on the small side, you will use these small diameter circular knitting techniques frequently.

Using Double-Pointed Needles

The first useful tool for knitting small-diameter tubes are double-pointed needles (abbreviated dpns), which are sold in packs of five. When you use them, you have three or four needles spanning the circumference of the tube that you're working on, holding the stitches that form your tube. You use an extra needle to do the actual knitting.

To begin knitting a tube on double-pointed needles, cast on the required number of stitches that form the initial circumference of your tube onto a single needle. Then divide these stitches evenly onto three or four double pointed needles and arrange the needles in a circle, being careful not to twist your stitches (1). Use an extra needle and the yarn coming from the final stitch that you cast on to begin working the first cast on stitch, the first stitch of your round.

A great way to keep your first stitch firmly attached to your final stitch in your circle is to knit the first three stitches of your round with both your working yarn and the long yarn tail from your cast-on stitches (2). Knit the rest of the stitches from needle one, using only the working yarn. Use the empty needle to continue knitting the stitches on the next needle in your round (3). Continue in this manner, and you'll soon have a tube-shaped piece of knitting (4). Voilà!

Knitting a tube with double-pointed needles

Using Two Circular Needles

Another great way to knit small-diameter tubes is by using two circular needles. Though this method still has an aura of unconventionality about it, it's a technique that's definitely worked its way into the mainstream of knitting. When you knit a tube on two circular needles, you work from only one needle at a time, so you'll always have one working needle and one idle needle. Stitches on the resting circular needle hang loosely on the cable portion of the needle.

To begin, cast on the stitches for the circumference of your tube onto one circular needle. Transfer half the stitches (beginning with the slipknot) onto the second circular needle, and slide these stitches to the opposite tip of that needle. Slide the stitches on needle one to the center of the needle cable, and drop needle one (1). Using the free tip of needle two, join the stitches into a round, working the first three stitches of your round with both the working yarn and the yarn tail from the cast-on end held together (2). Finish knitting the rest of the stitches on that needle, using only the working yarn. Then slide all the stitches on needle two to the center of the needle cable. Drop needle two and pick up needle one. Push the stitches from the cable to the tip of the needle (3).

Then, using the opposite end of needle one, knit all the stitches on that needle. Drop needle one and pick up needle two. Continue this process, alternating between needles, until you've finished your tube (4).

Knitting a tube with two circular needles

How to Choose?

So, which method of small-diameter circular knitting should you use? There are pros and cons to each method. Working with double-pointed needles can be awkward on very small tubes, and the needles sometimes slide off when they are holding only two or three stitches. With double-pointed needles, you also have to consciously snug up the stitches when going from one needle to the next to avoid loose stitches at the intersections. Knitting tubes on two circular needles is less awkward, and you usually don't need to worry about loose intersections, but constantly pushing the stitches back and forth on the cables can be very time-consuming. My recommendation is to learn both methods and discover the method that's more comfortable for your hands.

Knitting the Ropes: I-cord!

Some tubes can be knit using only two double-pointed needles. These tubes are known as idiot cord, referred to in genteel knitting society as merely I-cord. Any tube that has five stitches or less in circumference can be worked as I-cord.

Cast on or pick up the required number of stitches on a double-pointed needle. Knit the stitches with another double-pointed needle, but don't turn the work. Slide the stitches to the opposite end of the needle (1). Pull the working yarn tight across the back of the stitches (2) and knit another row. Repeat this many times, forming a tiny knitted tube (3). To keep the stitches looking uniform, tug on the tube every few rows.

I-cord

Pick Up Those Stitches!

Picking up stitches from one piece to begin another piece is a common technique used in many types of knitting. When knitting a sweater, for example, a common technique for creating a collar is to pick up stitches from the neck opening. When knitting amigurumi, we often create one or two constituent shapes and then, picking up stitches from both of these shapes, begin to build another shape to round out our form.

Picking up stitches allows you to avoid the pain of seaming many small pieces together. It also allows you to create amigurumi by building it up with a series of simpler shapes, eventually coming together into a complex whole. It can even be addicting, once you learn how to pick up stitches and realize how fun it is. So, let's get to it!

The Basics

The most confusing thing about picking up stitches is the technical jargon itself. What does it mean to "pick up stitches"? If you look at it literally, it seems as though the stitches are already there, and you simply need to pick them up (put them onto your needle) and you're all set. In reality, you cast on stitches directly onto your piece of knitting. To do this, slip your right needle into an available hole along the indicated edge, wrap your yarn around your needle (1), and pull a loop through onto your right needle (2). Now you've picked up one stitch. Continue in this manner across the edge (or middle) of your work until you've picked up the required number of stitches.

Picking up stitches

Here are a couple tips about picking up stitches: First, don't insert your needle through a strand of yarn, thereby splitting it. Second, don't pick up a stitch through a large hole. This will create an even larger hole.

The way you pick up stitches also varies slightly depending on where you are picking up your stitches: from a cast-on or bound-off edge, from a selvedge, or from the middle of your fabric.

From a Cast-On Edge

To pick up stitches from a cast-on edge, pick up one stitch per column of stitches. There are two ways to pick up stitches from a cast-on edge. You can pick up stitches invisibly from a cast-on edge by poking your needle between each column directly underneath the yarn strands of the cast-on edge itself. This will basically erase any line of demarcation between the old stitches and the new ones you are picking up (1).

You can also pick up stitches by poking your needle through the loops that are on the other side of the straight edge. This will create a neat line demarcating the edge itself, and is often useful for decorative purposes, where creating a clear line at the edge where you are picking up stitches is an important design element (2).

Picking up stitches from a cast-on edge

From a Bound-Off Edge

Picking up stitches from a bound-off edge is almost identical to picking them up from a cast-on edge. Pick up one stitch for every column of stitches on your edge. Pick up stitches invisibly from your edge, or pick them up in such a way that you create a clear demarcating line where you've picked up stitches.

Picking up stitches from a bound-off edge

From a Selvedge

When knitting in stockinette, the stitches are wider than they are tall. So, picking up stitches along a selvedge requires that you pick up approximately three stitches for every four rows along the edge. How to pick up stitches from your selvedge varies, depending on what type of selvedge you have. In most amigurumi knitting designs, selvedges are either a chain selvedge, created by slipping the first stitch of every row, or a garter selvedge, created by knitting or purling the first stitch of every row.

Chain selvedge

Garter selvedge

When you're picking up stitches along a chain selvedge, you will have two rows of stitches per link in your chain. Pick up your stitches as follows: pick up one stitch in between chains, one stitch at the chain, and another stitch in between chains. Then, skip the next chain and begin again. Notice the groups of three. With this method, the picked-up stitches will be tightly attached to your selvedge.

Picking up stitches along a chain selvedge

In a garter selvedge, you have one knot per two rows of knitting. To maintain the three-to-four ratio, pick up one stitch between knots, one stitch at a knot, another stitch between knots, and then skip the next knot. The spaces between the knots, as well as the knots themselves, are pretty tight, so as long as you pick up three stitches per four rows of knitting, the junction between your selvedge and your new stitches should be relatively hole-free.

Picking up stitches along a garter selvedge

From the Middle of Your Work

The way to pick up stitches on the middle of your work varies depending on the orientation of the stitches you need to pick up. If you're picking up stitches across columns of stitches, use the tip of your needle to reach into the stitch itself and lift up the running yarn from the wrong side. Pick up one stitch per column of stitches.

Picking up stitches across columns

When you're picking up stitches across rows of stitches, remember the three-to-four ratio. You should pick up only three stitches per four rows.

Picking up stitches across rows

In all the previous methods the stitches are picked up knitwise, from the right side of the work in a knit-like manner. There's another way to pick up stitches that's a little awkward but, nevertheless, will rear its fussy head from time to time: picking up stitches purlwise. In this method, you pick them up from the wrong side of the work in a purl-like manner.

With the wrong side (purl side) facing you and the yarn in front of the work, insert the needle from back to front through the appropriate hole, wrap the yarn around the needle, and pull a loop through onto your right needle. Repeat to pick up the indicated number of stitches.

Picking up stitches purlwise

Seaming

Seaming is necessary in nearly any sort of knitting, and amigurumi knitting is no exception. Even if we pick up stitches wherever possible, and almost always knit in the round, seams are pesky things that creep up where you least expect them. Consider yourself lucky if your amigurumi project calls for only one seam. In most situations, you'll have several different seams to deal with before you finish your critter.

The following types of seaming are the most common types found in amigurumi projects.

Whip Stitch

This is a simple stitch that is familiar to seamstresses, tailors, and surgeons. Unlike most seams in knitting, which are very cleverly executed to avoid detection by the discerning eye, a seam that is whip stitched is meant to be seen. This also makes it one of the easiest seams in all of knitting to work.

To whip stitch a seam, hold the pieces with wrong sides facing each other, and push your threaded needle through both pieces. Take the next stitch close to the first one, inserting the needle from the same side as the first stitch. The yarn will wrap over the top of the seam. Repeat to the end of the seam.

Whip stitch seam

Mattress Stitch

Mattress stitch is an invisible seaming stitch, useful for attaching two pieces together by their selvedges. Lay the pieces edge to edge, right side up. Hook your threaded tapestry needle under the first running yarn between the selvedge and the first column of stitches on one of the pieces.

Then, insert your needle under the first running yarn between the first column of stitches and selvedge on the second piece. Zigzag back and forth like this, catching every row in turn.

Leave the stitches fairly loose. After every few stitches, gently pull the yarn to tighten the seam and bring the edges together.

Note: When seaming a sweater with mattress stitch, you usually catch two rows with each stitch. For amigurumi, I recommend hooking every row to make an invisible seam.

Mattress stitch seam

Fake Grafting

Fake grafting allows you to connect cast-on edges to bound-off edges, cast-on edges to other cast-on edges, and bound-off edges to other bound-off edges. To begin, place the pieces edge to edge, right side up. Hook the needle around the first column of stitches in the first piece and, subsequently, under the first column of stitches in the second piece. Continue in this manner. Note that when you hook the needle under a column of stitches, the column must "point" toward the seam itself. In other words, hook the needle around the base of a knit stitch (bottom of the V) rather than around the top of the knit stitch (the top of the V).

Fake grafting

Combination Seaming

Pieces do not always align columns to columns or rows to rows. Often you need to seam two pieces together with rows to columns. In these cases, use a combination of mattress stitch and fake grafting to attach the pieces together.

Combination seam

Kitchener Stitch

Kitchener stitch, also known as grafting, is the seaming method of choice when you need to join a row of live stitches to a second row of live stitches. It produces an invisible seam that's virtually undetectable to any but the most expert of knitters. When you graft live stitches together via Kitchener stitch, the seam has the same thickness and elasticity as a normal line of knit stitches. You use your tapestry needle to guide the yarn through the live stitches in a way that replicates the path your yarn would follow in a normal row of stitches.

Cut the working yarn, leaving a tail about 18" (46 cm) long. Leave the stitches on the needles; there should be the same number of stitches on each. Hold the needles side by side in the left hand, with the right sides facing out. Slide the stitches toward the needle tips.

The working yarn will be coming from the first stitch on the back needle. To help demonstrate the steps, a contrasting yarn has been used in the photos. Thread the yarn tail on a yarn needle. Draw the yarn through the first stitch on the front needle as if to purl, and leave the stitch on the needle (1).

Keeping the yarn under the needles, draw the yarn through the first stitch on the back needle as if to knit, and leave the stitch on the needle (2).

* Draw the yarn through the first stitch on the front needle as if to knit, and slip the stitch off the needle (3). Draw the yarn through the next stitch on the front needle as if to purl, and leave the stitch on the needle.

Draw the yarn through the first stitch on the back needle as if to purl, and slip the stitch off the needle (4). Draw the yarn through the next stitch on the back needle as if to knit, and leave the stitch on the needle.

Repeat from * until all but the last two stitches have been worked off the needles. Insert the tapestry needle knitwise into the stitch on the front needle, and purlwise into the stitch on the back needle, slipping both stitches off their respective needles. Stretch out your seam or use the tip of a needle to adjust stitches a bit to even out the tension in the yarn (5).

Kitchener stitch

Loose Ends: Miscellaneous Tips, Tricks & Techniques

There are a few odds and ends of information that definitely belong in a book on amigurumi knitting, but don't necessarily apply to other kinds of knitting. Be sure to browse this section for useful tips, tricks, and techniques that will help you along in your amigurumi knitting adventures.

Amigurumi Gauge Sense

In amigurumi knitting, gauge sense is a little bit different from what it is in most other types of knitting. When you're knitting items that are to be worn, a precise gauge is essential. A gauge that varies by even a quarter of a stitch per inch can result in a finished garment that's inches too large or small. Since amigurumi doesn't really need to fit anybody, however, you're not obligated to work at any particular gauge. In that sense, gauge requirements when knitting amigurumi are much less stringent than they are when knitting sweaters, hats, and other types of clothing.

There is one extremely important aspect, however, in which gauge is crucial in amigurumi knitting. At some point, most amigurumi critters are stuffed with fiberfill. If you don't want this fluffy white stuff poking out of your creation, it's extremely important that you knit at a gauge that's tight for the weight of yarn that you're using. Let's take worsted weight yarn, for example. If you're working a sweater or hat with worsted weight yarn, it's pretty standard to knit it at a gauge of 4 stitches per inch (2.5 cm).

If you knit amigurumi with worsted weight yarn at this gauge, however, your knitted fabric will just look like a thin mesh that's barely holding giant wads of fiberfill at bay. To work amigurumi in worsted weight yarn, it's much more appropriate to work at a much tighter gauge. A gauge of 5.5 to 6 stitches per inch (2.5 cm) would do very nicely.

Since you'll need to work at a gauge that's significantly tighter than the gauge normally recommended for the yarn you're using, you'll need to use a needle that's much smaller than what you'd normally use. Instead of using the size 7 to size 9 (4.5 to 5.5 mm) needles normally recommended for worsted weight yarn, you'd use anywhere from a size 3 to a size 5 (3.25 to 3.75 mm) needle. If you're working with another weight of yarn, be sure to use a needle size that's approximately three to four sizes smaller than what you would typically use for that type of yarn.

A Word on Yarn

Like most knitters, I'm a fiber addict. It's probably the reason that I love to knit: it gives me an excuse to fondle scrumptious yarns for hours at a time. There are, however, a few considerations to take into account when choosing yarn for your amigurumi project.

One consideration is whether the yarn that you're using for your project is machine-washable or not. Though it's not much of an issue if you plan to display your amigurumi on your coffee table, it can become a problem if the critter is intended as a toy. Then it's probably a good idea to select a machine-washable yarn.

This way, you'll never be too upset when the critter that you've labored over for hours accidentally ends up in the toilet or a mud puddle.

Another thing to ponder is the type of fiber to use. Some fibers, namely wool, have a lot of memory. This means that once you've knitted them up and stuffed them with fiberfill, they'll maintain their cute three-dimensional form quite nicely. Other fibers, like angora, alpaca, cotton, and bamboo, don't have the same elasticity as wool. These are fibers that enjoy draping much more than they like hugging. Amigurumi made in these types of fibers are more likely to lose their shape over time, becoming more and more blob-like as the months pass. To avoid this, it's best to work your amigurumi in a fiber that has some memory to it. Wool blends are a great compromise in this situation: though they have some of the elasticity and memory of wool, they also contain other fibers that vary the quality of the knitted fabric.

A final consideration when working amigurumi is the weight of the yarn that you use. Since most amigurumi requires lots of shaping maneuvers, it's probably a good idea to begin working amigurumi in a multi-ply worsted weight wool yarn. Such yarn is relatively easy to manipulate with your needles, can be worked in a tight gauge, produces clear stitch definition, and is relatively easy on hands. One of my favorite yarns is Cascade 220, 100% Peruvian Highland Wool, 220 yards (201 m) per 3.5 oz (100 g) skein. This is the yarn used for each of the projects in this book. In addition to having all of the above qualities, it also has one of the most extensive color cards I've ever seen for a commercial yarn. Cascade 220 is not machine washable, however.

Regardless, multi-ply worsted weight yarns are everywhere. Find your favorite, and it'll become your amigurumi workhorse. After you've gotten a few creatures under your belt, you can move on to other exotic yarns.

Taking Care of Yarn Tails

In many knitting patterns, you'll find this obligatory final line: "Weave in yarn ends." This simple statement is enough to strike dread into the heart of many a knitter, who envision themselves, for days on end, using their tapestry needle to weave in the millions of yarn tails trailing from their nearly-finished work.

When you knit amigurumi, on the other hand, you don't need to feel such gloom. In most cases, the wrong side of the work will be utterly unreachable, nestled within a dark, comfortable bed of fiberfill. Therefore, the wrong side of your work doesn't need to be pretty and snag-free. Most of the time, you won't have to spend hours securing yarn ends to the wrong side of your work.

Here's a simple recipe for dealing with any yarn tails that you have in your work. First, take any yarn tails emerging on the wrong side of the work and shove them into the body of your work while you are stuffing. Once you've stuffed and closed up your piece, use your tapestry needle to thread any other yarn ends emerging from the right side of your work through the stuffed body of the piece. Then, simply snip the yarn tail at the point where it emerges from the body of the work.

Sometimes, you will have yarn tails that you really do need to secure. In such cases, you have two options. First, if you haven't closed up the piece yet, you can always do the tried-and-true: use your tapestry needle to weave the yarn end into the wrong side of the work. If, however, you've already closed up your critter, but still have some yarn ends that need securing, here's an excellent way to do it. First, use your tapestry needle to thread the yarn end through the body of the work. Then, thread another yarn end (which may or may not need securing) through the body of the work, making it emerge from the same point as the first yarn end. Then, tie these yarn ends together with a secure square knot. Then, thread each one into your tapestry needle in turn, and thread it through the body of the critter again, allowing each to emerge at an opposite end of your critter. Finally, finish off by snipping each yarn end at the point that it emerges from your work.

A Special Note on Toy Safety

Most kids love amigurumi, and there's little doubt that many of you will be knitting up the projects in this book for the wee ones in your lives. On that note, here are some important points to consider when making amigurumi critters for children.

First, be especially wary of giving children toys that have plastic eyes, noses, and other parts that can easily come off. Knitting, in general, is not well-suited for such knickknacks. By its very elastic nature, the knitted fabric is too loose to reliably hold notions like this into the work. If in doubt, err on the side of caution and use safer methods for detailing your critter. You can easily embroider most facial features for your critter, or knit them up and sew them on.

Another important consideration is the use of the chenille stems used in many of the projects. While chenille stems are fantastic for making the limbs of your various critters moldable, they are not so fantastic when it comes to children. Because knitted fabric is relatively loose even when it's worked at a tight gauge, it doesn't take much vigorous play to lead to an exposed chenille stem protruding wildly from an amigurumi creature. And, of course, children and sharp wires don't mix well. For the safety of all involved, I highly recommend that you don't use chenille stems in amigurumi pieces that are going to be toys for children.

Five Servings a Day:
the vegetable basket

Knitting veggies is a good place to start because most of them are pretty easy to do. They don't have arms or legs or faces to fret about. While you're knitting up a healthy basketful of veggies, you'll get lots of practice in shaping your knitting with increases and decreases and working in the round.

Aubergine

Strangely, the word *aubergine* sounds more delicious to me than its colloquial counterpart. Whichever name you prefer, these luscious culinary treats are revered in many cuisines for their flavor and versatility. This knit version provides an excellent introduction to picking up stitches and knitting in the round and is an essential addition to any basket of vegetables.

yarn

Worsted weight
MC (eggplant): 75 yd (69 m)
Shown: Cascade 220 color #7807
CC (deep green): 50 yd (46 m)
Shown: Cascade 220 #9430

needles

- One set U.S. size 5 (3.75 mm) double-pointed needles
  and/or
- Two U.S. size 5 (3.75 mm) circular needles,
  24" (61 cm) long

notions

- Fiberfill stuffing
- Tapestry needle

gauge

22 to 24 sts = 4" (10 cm) in stockinette stitch

dimensions

Diameter: 4½" (11.5 cm)
Length: 8" (20.3 cm)

difficulty

Beginner/Intermediate

Pattern

Leaves (Make 5)

In CC, CO 17 sts. Continue, working back and forth in rows, as follows:

Row 1 (wrong side): Sl1, [P1, K1] 7 times, P2.

Row 2 (right side): Sl1, [K1, P1] 3 times, Sl2-K1-P2SSO, [P1, K1] 3 times, P1—15 sts.

Row 3: Sl1, [P1, K1] 6 times, P2.

Row 4: Sl1, [K1, P1] 2 times, K1, Sl2-K1-P2SSO, K1, [P1, K1] 2 times, P1—13 sts.

Row 5: Sl1, [P1, K1] 2 times, P3, [K1, P1] 2 times, P1.

Row 6: Sl1, [K1, P1] 2 times, Sl2-K1-P2SSO, [P1, K1] 2 times, P1—11 sts.

Row 7: Sl1, [P1, K1] 4 times, P2.

Row 8: Sl1, K1, P1, K1, Sl2-K1-P2SSO, K1, P1, K1, P1—9 sts.

Row 9: Sl1, P1, K1, P3, K1, P2.

Row 10: Sl1, K1, P1, Sl2-K1-P2SSO, P1, K1, P1—7 sts.

Row 11: Sl1, [P1, K1] 2 times, P2.

Row 12: Sl1, K1, Sl2-K1-P2SSO, K1, P1—5 sts.

Row 13: Sl1, P4.

Row 14: Sl1, Sl2-K1-P2SSO, P1—3 sts.

Row 15: Sl1, P2.

Row 16: Sl2-K1-P2SSO—1 st.

Cut yarn, thread through final st and pull tight.

Leaf Assembly and Stem

Using CC, pick up 14 sts across the CO edge of each of the five leaves for a total of 70 sts. See **Figure 1** for guidance in picking up these sts.

Figure 1

Join these sts into a round, and proceed:

Round 1: *SSK, K10, K2tog, repeat from * to end of round—60 sts.

Round 2: *SSK, K8, K2tog, repeat from * to end of round—50 sts.

Round 3: *SSK, K6, K2tog, repeat from * to end of round—40 sts.

Round 4: *SSK, K4, K2tog, repeat from * to end of round—30 sts.

Round 5: *SSK, K2, K2tog, repeat from * to end of round—20 sts.

Round 6: *SSK, K2tog, repeat from * to end of round—10 sts.

Rounds 7–15: Knit.

Round 16: *K2tog, repeat from * to end of round—5 sts.

Cut yarn, thread through final 5 sts and pull tight. Using tapestry needle, thread this yarn end back through the tip of the stem to give it a blunt look.

Body

From the underside of the leaf and stem assembly, pick up a total of 40 sts in MC. Pick up these sts at the CO edge of the leaves. You will be picking up approximately 8 sts on the CO edge of each leaf. See **Figure 2** for guidance in picking up these sts.

Figure 2

Join these 40 sts into a round and continue:

Rounds 1–16: Knit.

Round 17: *K1, M1L, K7, repeat from * to end of round—45 sts.

Round 18: Knit.

Round 19: *K1, M1L, K8, repeat from * to end of round—50 sts.

Round 20: Knit.

Round 21: *K1, M1L, K9, repeat from * to end of round—55 sts.

Round 22: Knit.

Round 23: *K1, M1L, K10, repeat from * to end of round—60 sts.

Round 24: Knit.

Round 25: *K1, M1L, K11, repeat from * to end of round—65 sts.

Round 26: Knit.

Round 27: *K1, M1L, K12, repeat from * to end of round—70 sts.

Round 28: Knit.

Round 29: *K1, M1L, K13, repeat from * to end of round—75 sts.

Rounds 30–36: Knit.

Round 37: *K13, K2tog, repeat from * to end of round—70 sts.

Round 38: *K12, K2tog, repeat from * to end of round—65 sts.

Round 39: *K11, K2tog, repeat from * to end of round—60 sts.

Round 40: *K10, K2tog, repeat from * to end of round—55 sts.

Round 41: *K9, K2tog, repeat from * to end of round—50 sts.

Round 42: *K8, K2tog, repeat from * to end of round—45 sts.

Round 43: *K7, K2tog, repeat from * to end of round—40 sts.

Round 44: *K6, K2tog, repeat from * to end of round—35 sts.

Round 45: *K5, K2tog, repeat from * to end of round—30 sts.

Round 46: *K4, K2tog, repeat from * to end of round—25 sts.

Round 47: *K3, K2tog, repeat from * to end of round—20 sts.

Stuff the body of the eggplant with fiberfill. Do not overstuff! Continue:

Round 48: *K2, K2tog, repeat from * to end of round—15 sts.

Round 49: *K1, K2tog, repeat from * to end of round—10 sts.

Round 50: *K2tog, repeat from * to end of round—5 sts.

Cut yarn, thread through final 5 sts and pull tight.

Finishing

Sew the tips of the leaves to the side of the body. Take care of any loose yarn ends.

Tomato

Even in the middle of winter, tomatoes have a way of bringing back summer. This cute knit version is a great introduction to small diameter circular knitting, and makes a sleek, squishy ornament for your dining table year-round!

yarn
Worsted weight
MC (summer red): 50 yd (45.5 m)
Shown: Cascade 220 color #9466
CC (spring green): 20 yd (18 m)
Shown: Cascade 220 #7814

needles
• One set U.S. size 5 (3.75 mm) double-pointed needles
and/or
• Two U.S. size 5 (3.75 mm) circular needles,
20"–24" (51–61 cm) long

notions
• Fiberfill stuffing
• Tapestry needle

gauge
22 to 24 sts = 4" (10 cm) in stockinette stitch

dimensions
Diameter: 5" (12.7 cm)
Height: 3" (7.6 cm)

difficulty
Beginner/Intermediate

Pattern

Leaves *(make 5)*

CO 8 sts in CC. BO all sts. Thread yarn through final lp and pull tight. Weave in yarn ends.

Stem

Use CC yarn and pick up 2 sts from the blunt end of each of the five leaves, for a total of 10 stitches. See **Figure 1** for guidance.

Figure 1

Join these into a round and continue:

Round 1: Knit.

Round 2: [K2tog, K2tog, K1] 2 times—6 sts.

Round 3: K2tog 3 times—3 sts. Knit 1" (2.5 cm) of I-cord.

Cut yarn and thread through remaining 3 sts. Pull yarn end through the center of the stem to make a blunt end.

Body

Use MC yarn, and CO 4 stitches. Join these sts into a round and continue.

Rounds 1, 3, 5, 7, 9, 11, 13, 15: Knit.

Round 2: [K1, KLL, KRL, K1] 2 times—8 sts.

Round 4: [K1, KLL, K2, KRL, K1] 2 times—12 sts.

Round 6: [K1, KLL, K4, KRL, K1] 2 times—16 sts.

Round 8: [K1, KLL, K6, KRL, K1] 2 times—20 sts.

Round 10: [K1, KLL, K8, KRL, K1] 2 times—24 sts.

Round 12: *K1, KLL, K2, KRL, K1, repeat from * to end of round—36 sts.

Round 14: *K1, KLL, K4, KRL, K1, repeat from * to end of round—48 sts.

Round 16: *K1, KLL, K6, KRL, K1, repeat from * to end of round—60 sts.

Rounds 17–27: Knit.

Round 28: *K10, K2tog, repeat from * to end of round—55 sts.

Rounds 29 and 31: Knit.

Round 30: *K9, K2tog, repeat from * to end of round—50 sts.

Round 32: *K8, K2tog, repeat from * to end of round—45 sts.

Round 33: *K7, K2tog, repeat from * to end of round—40 sts.

Round 34: *K6, K2tog, repeat from * to end of round—35 sts.

Round 35: *K5, K2tog, repeat from * to end of round—30 sts.

Round 36: *K4, K2tog, repeat from * to end of round—25 sts.

Round 37: *K3, K2tog, repeat from * to end of round—20 sts.

Round 38: *K2, K2tog, repeat from * to end of round—15 sts.

Round 39: *K1, K2tog, repeat from * to end of round—10 sts.

Round 40: *K2tog 5 times. (5 stitches)

Lightly stuff the body with polyester stuffing. Do not overstuff! Cut yarn, thread through final 5 sts and pull tight.

Finishing

Thread the yarn tail from the CO edge through the body of the tomato, and pull firmly to create an indentation. See **Figure 2** for guidance. Secure this yarn tail. Sew leaves and stem onto the top portion of the body within this indentation. Take care of any loose yarn ends.

Figure 2

Carrot

This brilliant root vegetable is a wonderful source of beta-carotene, a relative of vitamin A. This knit version is an excellent exercise in short row knitting, with an intricate top created by utilizing a picot bind-off method. Knit a whole bunch to really brighten up your basket of veggies!

yarn
Worsted weight
MC (brilliant orange): 40 yd (37 m)
Shown: Cascade 220 color #9465B
CC (lively green): 40 yd (37 m)
Shown: Cascade 220 color #2409

needles
- One set U.S. size 5 (3.75 mm) double-pointed needles
and/or
- Two U.S. size 5 (3.75 mm) circular needles, 24" (61 cm) long

notions
- Fiberfill stuffing
- Tapestry needle

gauge
22 to 24 sts = 4" (10 cm) in stockinette stitch

dimensions
Length: 15" (38 cm)

difficulty
Beginner/Intermediate

Pattern

Root

In MC, CO 52 stitches. Continue, working back and forth in rows:

Row 1: Sl1, P44, w&t.

Row 2: K43, w&t.

Row 3: P37, w&t.

Row 4: K35, w&t.

Row 5: P32, w&t.

Row 6: K31, w&t.

Row 7: P37, w&t.

Row 8: K39, w&t.

Row 9: P45, w&t.

Row 10: K48.

Row 11: Sl1, P32, w&t.

Row 12: K27, w&t.

Row 13: P21, w&t.

Row 14: K23, w&t.

Row 15: P20, w&t.

Row 16: K21, w&t.

Row 17: P27, w&t.

Row 18: K25, w&t.

Row 19: P40, w&t.

Rows 20–26: Repeat rows 2–8.

Row 27: P48, K1.

Row 28: Sl1, K51.

Rows 29–37: Repeat rows 11–19.

Rows 38–54: Repeat rows 2–18.

Row 55: P46, K1.

Row 56: Sl1, K51.

Turn work. Using a second needle, pick up an additional 52 stitches along the CO edge of the work.

Cut yarn, leaving a long tail. Using tapestry needle and this long yarn tail, graft (Kitchener stitch) the 52 stitches from the original needle to the 52 stitches on the second needle.

While grafting, stuff the body of the carrot with fiberfill. Do not overstuff.

Top

Make four green fronds for your carrot top as follows.

In CC, CO x stitches, where x is equal to 20, 30, 35, and 40, respectively. Knit one row. Then BO y stitches, where y is equal to 16, 24, 28, and 32, as follows: BO one stitch; *transfer stitch back to the left needle and CO 5 stitches using the knit-on method; BO 7 stitches; repeat from * until you've bound off y stitches. Then, BO the remaining stitches in the conventional fashion.

Finishing

Sew each of the top fronds to the top of the carrot body. Take care of any loose yarn ends.

Garlic

This pungent bulb is a quick and simple knit, and yet another essential item for any veggie basket. For one thing, it'll give you great practice knitting in the round. Plus, who can resist those fiendishly cute root hairs?

yarn

Worsted weight
MC (natural white): 40 yd (37 m)
Shown: Cascade 220 color #8010

needles

· One set U.S. size 5 (3.75 mm) double-pointed needles
and/or
· Two U.S. size 5 (3.75 mm) circular needles,
 24" (61 cm) long

notions

· Fiberfill stuffing
· Tapestry needle

gauge

22 to 24 sts = 4" (10 cm) in stockinette stitch

dimensions

Length: 4" (10 cm)

difficulty

Beginner/Intermediate

Pattern

Body

In MC, CO 12 sts. Join these sts into a round and continue:

Round 1: Knit.

Round 2: [M1R, K1, M1L, K1] 6 times—24 sts.

Round 3: Knit.

Round 4: [K1, M1R, K1, M1L, K2] 6 time—36 sts.

Round 5: Knit.

Round 6: [K2, M1R, K1, M1L, K3] 6 times—48 sts.

Round 7: Knit.

Rounds 8–10: [K3, Sl1 purlwise, K4] 6 times.

Round 11: Knit.

Rounds 12–14: [K3, Sl1 purlwise, K4] 6 times.

Round 15: Knit.

Rounds 16–18: [K3, Sl1 purlwise, K4] 6 times.

Round 19: Knit.

Round 20: [K2, Sl2-K1-P2SSO, K3] 6 times—36 sts.

Rounds 21–23: [K2, Sl1 purlwise, K3] 6 times.

Round 24: Knit.

Round 25: [K1, Sl2-K1-P2SSO, K2] 6 times—24 sts.

Rounds 26–28: [K1, Sl1 purlwise, K2] 6 times.

Round 29: Knit.

Round 30: [Sl2-K1-P2SSO, K1] 6 times—12 sts.

Rounds 31 & 32: Knit.

Round 33: K2tog 6 times—6 sts.

Rounds 34–36: Knit.

Round 37: [K2tog, K1] 2 times—4 sts.

Rounds 38–40: Knit.

Round 41: K2tog, K2—3 sts.

Rounds 42 & 43: Knit.

Round 44: K2tog, K1—2 sts.

Stuff the body of the garlic bulb with fiberfill. Do not overstuff.

Cut yarn, thread through final 2 sts, and pull tight.

Root Hairs

Use MC to pick up 12 sts around the CO edge of the work. Join these sts into a round and continue:

Round 1: Purl.

Round 2: P2tog 6 time—6 sts.

Round 3: Knit.

Stuff the body of the garlic with any extra fiberfill, as desired. Continue:

Round 4: P2tog 3 times—3 sts.

Cut yarn, thread through final 3 sts, and pull tight. Thread this yarn end through the body of the work.

Cut several short (2" [5 cm]) lengths of MC yarn. Separate the plies of each to obtain fine, single-ply strands. Use a tapestry needle to thread these single-ply lengths of yarn through each of the purl bumps on the underside of the work. Secure each by tying a secure square knot. Fluff and clip the root hairs, as necessary.

Finishing

Take care of any loose yarn ends.

Cucumber

This refreshing vegetable is another summer staple. In addition to brightening your vegetable basket, it will allow you to practice small diameter circular knitting as well as color stranding techniques.

yarn

Worsted weight
MC (evergreen): 30 yd (27.5 m)
Shown: Cascade 220 color #9430
CC (chartreuse): 25 yd (23 m)
Shown: Cascade 220 color #8902

needles

- One set U.S. size 5 (3.75 mm) double-pointed needles
  and/or
- Two U.S. size 5 (3.75 mm) circular needles, 24" (61 cm) long

notions

- Fiberfill stuffing
- Tapestry needle

gauge

22 to 24 sts = 4" (10 cm) in stockinette stitch

dimensions

Length: 8½" (21.5 cm)

difficulty

Beginner/Intermediate

Pattern

Begin

In MC, CO 4 sts. Join these sts in a round and continue:

Round 1: Knit.

Round 2: *K-fb, repeat from * to end of round—8 sts.

Round 3: Knit.

Round 4: *K1, KLL, repeat from * to end of round—16 sts.

Round 5: Knit.

Round 6: *K2, M1L repeat from * to end of round—24 sts.

Body

Attach CC. Continue with MC and CC yarns.

Rounds 7–47: *K1 in MC, K1 in CC, K2 in MC, repeat from * to end of round.

Round 48: *K1 in MC, K1 in CC, K2tog in MC, repeat from * to end of round—18 sts.

Round 49: *K1 in MC, K1 in CC, K1 in MC, repeat from * to end of round. Cut CC yarn. Stuff your vegetable with fiberfill. Continue in MC.

Round 50: *K1, K2tog, repeat from * to end of round—12 sts.

Round 51: Knit.

Round 52: * K2tog, repeat from * to end of round—6 sts.

Rounds 53 and 54: Knit.

Cut yarn, thread through final 4 sts, and pull tight.

Finishing

Take care of any remaining yarn ends.

Peas in a Pod

Fresh peas are among the most aesthetically pleasing of all vegetables. With their spring-colored pods and petite seeds, these delectable treats are essential ingredients in any vegetable basket. This project includes both a closed pod and an open pod.

yarn
Worsted weight
MC (spring green): 30 yd (27.5 m)
Shown: Cascade 220 color #8903
CC (chartreuse): 20 yd (18 m)
Shown: Cascade 220 color #8910

needles
• One set U.S. size 5 (3.75 mm) double-pointed needles
  and/or
• Two U.S. size 5 (3.75 mm) circular needles,
  24" (61 cm) long

notions
• Fiberfill stuffing
• Tapestry needle

gauge
22 to 24 sts = 4" (10 cm) in stockinette stitch

dimensions
Length of pod: 4" (10 cm)
Diameter of pea: ½" (1.3 cm)

difficulty
Beginner/Intermediate

Pattern

Sealed Pod

In MC, CO 4 sts. Join these sts into a round, and continue:

Rounds 1 & 2: Knit.

Round 3: [K1, KLL, KRL, K1] 2 times—8 sts.

Round 4: Knit.

Round 5: [K1, M1L, K2, M1R, K1] 2 times—12 sts.

Round 6: Knit.

Round 7: [K1, M1L, K4, M1R, K1] 2 times—16 sts.

Round 8: Knit.

Round 9: SSK, K5, M1R, K2, M1L, K5, K2tog—16 sts.

Round 10: Knit.

Rounds 11–32: Repeat rounds 9 & 10 eleven more times.

Round 33: SSK, K5, M1R, K2, M1L, K5, K2tog—16 sts.

Round 34: SSK, K12, K2tog—14 sts.

Round 35: SSK, K4, M1R, K2, M1L, K4, K2tog—14 sts.

Round 36: SSK, K10, K2tog—12 sts.

Round 37: SSK, K3, M1R, K2, M1L, K3, K2tog—12 sts.

Round 38: SSK, K8, K2tog—10 sts.

Round 39: SSK, K2, M1R, K2, M1L, K2, K2tog—10 sts.

Round 40: SSK, K6, K2tog—8 sts.

Round 41: SSK, K1, M1R, K2, M1L, K1, K2tog—8 sts.

Round 42: SSK, K4, K2tog—6 sts.

Stuff the body of the pod with fiberfill. Do not overstuff. Continue:

Round 43: SSK, M1R, K2, M1L, K2tog—6 sts.

Round 44: SSK, K2, K2tog—4 sts.

Round 45: SSK, K2tog—2 sts.

Cut yarn, thread through final 2 sts and pull tight.

Open Pod

In MC, CO 4 sts. Continue, working back and forth in rows:

Row 1: Sl1, P2, K1.

Row 2: Sl1, KRL, K2, KLL, K1—6 sts.

Row 3: Sl1, P4, K1.

Row 4: Sl1, [K1, KLL, KRL, K1] 2 times, K1—10 sts.

Row 5: Sl1, P8, K1.

Row 6: Sl1, [K1, M1L, K2, M1R, K1] 2 times, K1—14 sts.

Row 7: Sl1, P12, K1.

Row 8: Sl1, [K1, M1L, K4, M1R, K1] 2 times, K1—18 sts.

Row 9: Sl1, P16, K1.

Row 10: Sl1, SSK, K5, M1R, K2, M1L, K5, K2tog, K1—18 sts.

Row 11: Sl1, P16, K1.

Rows 12–33: Repeat rows 10 & 11 another 11 times.

Row 34: Repeat row 10.

Row 35: Sl1, P2tog, P12, P2tog-tbl, K1—16 sts.

Row 36: Sl1, SSK, K4, M1R, K2, M1L, K4, K2tog, K1—16 sts.

Row 37: Sl1, P2tog, P10, P2tog-tbl, K1—14 sts.

Row 38: Sl1, SSK, K3, M1R, K2, M1L, K3, K2tog, K1—14 sts.

Row 39: Sl1, P2tog, P8, P2tog-tbl, K1—12 sts.

Row 40: Sl1, SSK, K2, M1R, K2, M1L, K2, K2tog, K1—12 sts.

Row 41: Sl1, P2tog, P6, P2tog-tbl, K1—10 sts.

Row 42: Sl1, SSK, K1, M1R, K2, M1L, K1, K2tog, K1—10 sts.

Row 43: Sl1, P2tog, P4, P2tog-tbl, K1—8 sts.

Row 44: Sl1, SSK, M1R, K2, M1L, K2tog, K1—8 sts.

Row 45: Sl1, P2tog, P2, P2tog-tbl, K1—6 sts.

Row 46: Sl1, K2tog, SSK, K1—4 sts.

Row 47: Sl1, P2, K1.

Row 48: K2tog, SSK—2 sts.

Cut yarn, thread through remaining 2 sts and pull tight.

Peas

Work several peas (three to five, as desired) into the open pod as follows. Use CC yarn and pick up 8 sts in a circle at the midline of the inside of the pod. See **Figure 1** for guidance in picking up these stitches.

Figure 1

Join these sts into a round, and continue:

Round 1: Knit.

Round 2: [K1, KLL, KRL, K1] 4 times—16 sts.

Rounds 3-5: Knit.

Round 6: [K2, K2tog] 4 times—12 sts.

Round 7: [K1, K2tog] 4 times—8 sts.

Round 8: K2tog 4 times—4 sts.

Lightly stuff the pea with fiberfill. Cut yarn and thread through remaining 4 sts.

Finishing

Take care of any loose yarn ends. You're done!

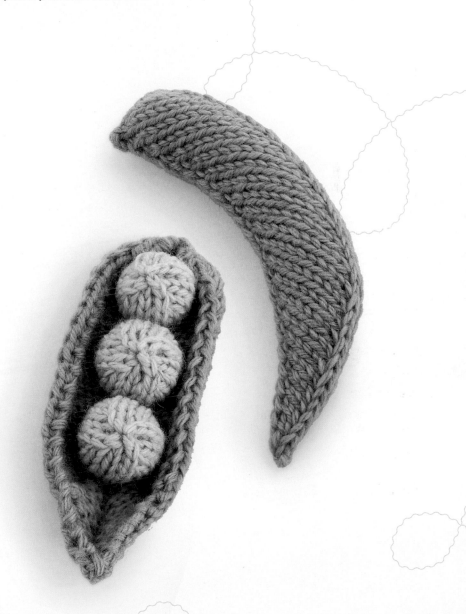

Get Your Barnacle On:

underwater creatures

We know more about the surface of the moon than we know about the deepest reaches of the oceans. Here is a generous sampling of oceanic amigurumi for your knitting pleasure, representing the myriad of fascinating creatures found in our planet's seas.

Hermit Crab

Hermit crabs are fascinating to watch at an aquarium. Because they are detritivores, they sift and eat in a continual flurry, their little mouthparts and legs moving with rapid-fire efficiency. This crab version is a lengthy project, requiring working knowledge of short rows, picking up stiches, Kitchener grafting, the knit cast-on method, increases, and decreases. The end result, though, is the sweetest knit crustacean you'll ever see!

yarn
Worsted weight
Shell Color 1 (SC1) (spring shoot green): 50 yd (46 m)
Shown: Cascade 220 color #8903
Shell Color 2 (SC2) (light cerulean blue): 50 yd (46 m)
Shown: Cascade 220 color #8908
Body Color 1 (BC1) (very coral): 60 yd (55 m)
Shown: Cascade 220 color #7830
Body Color 2 (BC2) (baby pink): 20 yd (18 m)
Shown: Cascade 220 color #4192
Eye Color (EC) (ebony): less than 5 yd (4.5 m)
Shown: Cascade 220 color #7822

needles
· One set U.S. size 5 (3.75 mm) double-pointed needles
and/or
· Two U.S. size 5 (3.75 mm) circular needles,
24" (61 cm) long

notions
· Fiberfill stuffing
· Tapestry needle
· Seven 12" (30.5 cm) chenille stems (optional)
· Stitch holder

gauge
22 to 24 sts = 4" (10 cm) in stockinette stitch

dimensions
Shell diameter: 5" (12.5 cm)

difficulty
Intermediate/
Experienced

Pattern

Shell

Using the knit cast-on method, CO 27 sts in SC1. Proceed as follows, working back and forth in rows:

Row 1: *K-tbl, repeat from * to end of row.

Row 2: Sl1 kwise, P1, w&t.

Row 3: K-fb, P1—28 sts.

Row 4: Sl1 kwise, P3, w&t.

Row 5: K-fb, K-fb, K1, P1—30 sts.

Row 6: Sl1 kwise, P6, w&t.

Row 7: K-fb, K-fb, K1, K-fb, K2, P1—33 sts.

Row 8: Sl1 kwise, P10, w&t.

Row 9: K-fb, K-fb, K1, K-fb, K2, K-fb, K3, P1—37 sts.

Cut SC1, and attach SC2. Continue:

Row 10: Sl1 kwise, P16, w&t.

Row 11: K-fb, K-fb, K-fb, K1, K-fb, K2, K-fb, K3, K-fb, K4, P1—43 sts.

Row 12: Sl1 kwise, P24, w&t.

Row 13: K-fb, K-fb, K-fb, K1, K-fb, K1, K-fb, K2, K-fb, K3, K-fb, K4, K-fb, K5, P1—51 sts.

Row 14: Sl1 kwise, P34, w&t.

Row 15: K-fb, K-fb, K-fb, K1, K-fb, K1, K-fb, K2, K-fb, K2, K-fb, K3, K-fb, K4, K-fb, K5, K-fb, K6, P1—61 sts.

Cut SC2, and reattach SC1. Continue:

Row 16: Sl1 kwise, P47, w&t.

Row 17: K-fb 3 times, [K-fb, K1] 2 times, [K-fb, K2] 2 times, [K-fb, K3] 2 times, K-fb, K4, K-fb, K5, K-fb, K6, K-fb, K7, P1—74 sts.

Row 18: Sl1 kwise, P63, w&t.

Row 19: K-fb 3 times, [K-fb, K1] 3 times, [K-fb, K2] 2 times, [K-fb, K3] 2 times, [K-fb, K4] 2 times, K-fb, K5, K-fb, K6, K-fb, K7, K-fb, K8, P1—90 sts.

Cut SC1, and reattach SC2. Continue:

Row 20: Sl1 kwise, P83, w&t.

Row 21: K-fb 4 times, [K-fb, K1] 3 times, [K-fb, K2] 3 times, [K-fb, K3] 2 times, [K-fb, K4] 2 times, [K-fb, K5] 2 times, K-fb, K6, K-fb, K7, K-fb, K8, K-fb, K9, P1—110 sts.

Cut SC2, and reattach SC1. Continue:

Row 22: Sl1 kwise, P108, K1.

Row 23: Sl1 kwise, K-fb 5 times, [K-fb, K1] 4 times, [K-fb, K2] 3 times, [K-fb, K3] 3 times, [K-fb, K4] 2 times, [K-fb, K5] 2 times, [K-fb, K6] 2 times, K-fb, K7, K-fb, K8, K-fb, K9, K-fb, K10, P1—135 sts.

Cut SC1. Place 135 stitches on a stitch holder for later use.

Now, use C2 yarn, and pick up 27 sts kwise from the CO edge of the work. Continue, working back and forth in rows as follows:

Row 1: *P-tbl, repeat from * to end of row.

Row 2: Sl1 kwise, K-fb, w&t—28 sts.

Row 3: P3.

Row 4: Sl1 kwise, K-fb, K1, K-fb, w&t—30 sts.

Row 5: P6.

Row 6: Sl1 kwise, K-fb, K2, K-fb, K1, K-fb, w&t—33 sts.

Row 7: P10.

Row 8: Sl1 kwise, K-fb, K3, K-fb, K2, K-fb, K1, K-fb, w&t—37 sts.

Row 9: P15.

Cut SC2, and attach SC1. Continue:

Row 10: Sl1 kwise, K-fb, K4, K-fb, K3, K-fb, K2, K-fb, K1, K-fb 2 times, w&t—43 sts.

Row 11: P23.

Row 12: Sl1 kwise, K-fb, K5, K-fb, K4, K-fb, K3, K-fb, K2, [K-fb, K1] 2 times, K-fb 2 times, w&t—51 sts.

Row 13: P33.

Row 14: Sl1 kwise, K-fb, K6, K-fb, K5, K-fb, K4, K-fb, K3, [K-fb, K2] 2 times, [K-fb, K1] 2 times, K-fb 2 times, w&t—61 sts.

Row 15: P45.

Cut SC1, and reattach SC2. Continue:

Row 16: Sl1 kwise, K-fb, K7, K-fb, K6, K-fb, K5, K-fb, K4, [K-fb, K3] 2 times, [K-fb, K2] 2 times, [K-fb, K1] 2 times, K-fb 3 times, w&t—74 sts.

Row 17: P61.

Row 18: Sl1 kwise, K-fb, K8, K-fb, K7, K-fb, K6, K-fb, K5, [K-fb, K4] 2 times, [K-fb, K3] 2 times, [K-fb, K2] 2 times, [K-fb, K1] 3 times, K-fb 3 times, w&t—90 sts.

Row 19: P80.

Cut SC2, and reattach SC1. Continue:

Row 20: Sl1 kwise, K-fb, K9, K-fb, K8, K-fb, K7, K-fb, K6, [K-fb, K5] 2 times, [K-fb, K4] 2 times, [K-fb, K3] 2 times, [K-fb, K2] 3 times, [K-fb, K1] 3 times, K-fb 4 times, w&t—110 sts.

Row 21: P104.

Cut SC1, and reattach SC2. Continue:

Row 22: Sl1 kwise, K-fb, K10, K-fb, K9, K-fb, K8, K-fb, K7, [K-fb, K6] 2 times, [K-fb, K5] 2 times, [K-fb, K4] 2 times, [K-fb, K3] 3 times, [K-fb, K2] 3 times, [K-fb, K1] 4 times, K-fb 5 times, K1—135 sts.

Cut yarn, leaving a long tail. Transfer 135 held sts from stitch holder to a second needle. Use a tapestry needle and graft (using Kitchener st) the 135 sts from the first needle to the 135 sts from the second needle. As you are grafting, carefully stuff the shell with fiberfill. For an additional corkscrew effect, fold a chenille stem in half, and place it on the inner corkscrew of the shell. Use this chenille stem to shape the inner spiral of the shell as you are stuffing. Weave in any yarn ends.

Chelipeds *(Make 2)*

In BC1, CO 37 sts. Continue, working back and forth in rows as follows:

Row 1 (wrong side): Sl1 kwise, P12, w&t.

Row 2: K11, w&t.

Row 3: P10, w&t.

Row 4: K9, w&t.

Row 5: P8, w&t.

Row 6: K7, w&t.

Row 7: P19, w&t.

Row 8: K9, w&t.

Row 9: P8, w&t.

Row 10: K7, w&t.

Row 11: P6, w&t.

Row 12: K5, w&t.

Row 13: P21.

Row 14: Sl1 kwise, K12, w&t.

Row 15: P13.

Row 16: Sl1 kwise, K11, w&t.

Row 17: P12.

Row 18: Sl1 kwise, K10, w&t.

Row 19: P11.

Row 20: Sl1 kwise, K9, w&t.

Row 21: P10.

Row 22: Sl1 kwise, P35, K1.

BO all sts as follows: *P2tog, transfer st back to left needle, continue from * until only 1 lp remains. Cut yarn, thread through final st, and pull tight.

Using BC1, whip st the first 4 sts from the CO edge to the first 4 sts of the BO edge. Next, use BC2 and pick up 32 sts from the BO edge of the work. Turn work. Continue along CO edge and pick up another 32 sts using BC2. See **Figure 1** for guidance.

Figure 1

Cut BC2 yarn, leaving a long tail. Using a tapestry needle and this yarn tail, graft (Kitchener st) the sts picked up from the CO edge to the sts picked up from the BO edge. While you are grafting, lightly stuff the cheliped with fiberfill.

If desired, place a folded chenille stem inside the cheliped while you are stuffing and grafting. This will allow you to pose the chelipeds of your finished creature.

To work the pincer of the cheliped, use BC1 yarn, and pick up 6 sts from the side of the cheliped. Turn the work, and pick up another 6 sts from the opposite side of the cheliped, for a total of 12 sts. You will be picking up the sts close to the tip of the cheliped near the intersection of the first and second segments. Use **Figure 2** for guidance.

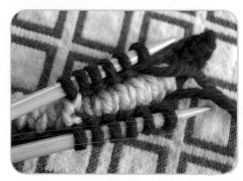

Figure 2

Continue, working in rounds, as follows:

Round 1: K4, K2tog, SSK, K4—10 sts.

Round 2: K1, M1L, K2, K2tog, SSK, K2, M1R, K1—10 sts.

Round 3: K3, K2tog, SSK, K3—8 sts.

Round 4: K1, M1L, K1, K2tog, SSK, K1, M1R, K1—8 sts.

Round 5: K2, K2tog, SSK, K2—6 sts.

Lightly stuff the pincer with fiberfill.

Round 6: K1, M1L, K2tog, SSK, M1R, K1—6 sts.

Round 7: K1, K2tog, SSK, K1—4 sts.

Cut yarn, thread through final 4 sts and pull tight.

Legs *(Make 4)*

In BC1, CO 31 sts. Continue, working in rows, as follows:

Row 1 (wrong side): Sl1 kwise, P9, w&t.

Row 2: K7, w&t.

Row 3: P6, w&t.

Row 4: K4, w&t.

Row 5: P15, w&t.

Row 6: K9, w&t.

Row 7: P8, w&t.

Row 8: K7, w&t.

Row 9: P6, w&t.

Row 10: K5, w&t.

Row 11: P18.

Row 12: Sl1 kwise, K9, w&t.

Row 13: P10.

Row 14: Sl1 kwise, K8, w&t.

Row 15: P9.

Row 16: Sl1 kwise, K7, w&t.

Row 17: P8.

Row 18: Sl1 kwise, K6, w&t.

Row 19: P7.

Row 20: Sl1 kwise, P29, K1.

BO sts as follows: *P2tog, transfer st to left needle, repeat from * until only 1 lp remains. Cut yarn, thread through final st, and pull tight. Using BC1, whip st the first 10 sts of the cast-on edge to the BO edge. Now, use BC2 to pick up 20 sts from the CO edge. Continuing with the same yarn, pick up another 20 sts from the BO edge, for a total of 40 sts. Pick up these sts from the lps just inside of the CO or BO edge. This will create a clean demarcation between the carapace of the limb and its underside. Your leg should now resemble **Figure 3**.

Figure 3

Divide these 40 sts evenly onto 2 needles. Cut yarn, leaving a long tail. Using a tapestry needle and this long tail, graft (Kitchener st) the sts from the first needle to the sts on the second needle. While doing this, lightly stuff the leg. For a pose-able leg, fold a chenille stem in half and twist securely. Insert this, blunt end first, into the leg, and stuff fiberfill around this as you are grafting.

Assembly of Legs

Using **Figure 4** for guidance, sew the four legs into the open end of the shell. Using **Figure 5** for guidance, sew the two chelipeds into the open end of the shell, allowing them to rest atop the legs.

Figure 4

Figure 5

Head

CO 25 sts in BC1. Join these sts into a round and continue:

Rounds 1–3: Knit.

Round 4: SSK, K11, K2tog, SSK, K6, K2tog—21 sts.

Round 5: Knit.

Round 6: SSK, K9, K2tog, SSK, K4, K2tog—17 sts.

Round 7: Knit.

Round 8: SSK, K2, Sl2-K1-P2SSO, K2, K2tog, SSK, K2, K2tog—11 sts.

Round 9: Knit.

Round 10: SSK, Sl2-K1-P2SSO, K2tog, SSK, K2tog—5 sts.

Rounds 11 & 12: Knit.

Round 13: Sl2-K1-P2SSO, K2—3 sts.

Cut yarn, thread through final 3 sts and pull tight.

Whiskers

Work the base of the left whisker as follows. Using BC1, pick up 4 sts on the decrease line on the left side of the head. To pick these sts up, start near the pointed tip of the face, and pick up one st on every row, working along the decrease line. Turn the work, and pick up another 4 sts on the decrease line behind the first 4 sts. Use **Figure 6** for guidance in picking up these 8 sts. Join these stitches in a round and proceed:

Figure 6

Round 1: Knit.

Round 2: K2, K2tog, SSK, K2—6 sts.

Round 3: K1, K2tog, SSK, 1—4 sts.

Round 4: K2tog, SSK—2 sts.

Cut yarn, leaving a 3" (7.5 cm) tail. Thread this yarn tail through the remaining 2 sts and pull tight. Using your tapestry needle, break apart the plies of this yarn to create the whiskers on the left side of the face.

Work the base of the right whisker analogously by picking up sts on the right side of the head.

Eyestalks

Work the left eyestalk as follows. Pick up 3 sts on the top of the left side of the head as shown in **Figure 7**. Note that the sts are picked up in a ring on the left side of the head, very close to the tip of the snout.

Figure 7

Join these sts into a round and proceed:

Rounds 1–7: Knit.

Round 8: K-fb 3 times—6 sts.

Rounds 9 & 10: Knit.

Cut BC1 yarn, and attach EC yarn. Continue:

Rounds 11–13: Knit.

Cut yarn, thread through remaining 6 sts, and pull tight.

Work the right eyestalk analogously by picking up sts on the right side of the head.

Final Assembly and Finishing

Stuff the head with fiberfill. Sew the head into the opening of the shell, above the legs and chelipeds. Be sure to sew the CO edge of the head to the inside of the lip of the shell. This will give the illusion that your little crab is peeking out of his shell. Before you finish sewing, be sure that you have adequately stuffed your creation. Take care of any loose yarn ends.

Common Octopus

Octopuses are among my favorite invertebrates. This knit version is a real tactile treat. Not only is it soft and huggable, but the arms can be made pose-able by the use of chenille stems, making for hours of cephalopod-filled fun!

yarn

Worsted weight
MC (blood red): 75 yd (68.5 m)
Shown: Cascade 220 color #9404
CC (deep yellow): 25 yd (23 m)
Shown: Cascade 220 color #9463B
Small amounts of natural white and dark brown for embroidering eyes

needles

- One set U.S. size 5 (3.75 mm) double-pointed needles
  and/or
- Two U.S. size 5 (3.75 mm) circular needles, 24" (61 cm) long

notions

- Eight 12" (30.5 cm) chenille stems
- Fiberfill stuffing
- Tapestry needle

gauge

22 to 24 sts = 4" (10 cm) in stockinette stitch

dimensions

Diameter: 7" (18 cm)
Height: 4" (10 cm)
Mantle length: 5" (12.5 cm)

difficulty

Intermediate/Experienced

Pattern

Tentacles *(Make 8)*

In CC, CO 28 sts.

Switch to MC.

Row 1 (Right side): K28.

Row 2: P14, w&t.

Row 3: K14.

Row 4: P21, w&t.

Row 5: K21.

Row 6: P7, w&t.

Row 7: K7.

Row 8: P28.

Switch to back to CC.

Row 9: K28.

BO all sts. Leave a long tail of yarn and thread through lp. Pull tight.

Use tapestry needle and whip st CO edge to BO edge with long tail of yarn.

Mantle and Head

CO 4 sts in MC. Divide onto 4 dpns or 2 circular needles. Join into a round.

Round 1: Knit.

Round 2: *KRL, K1, repeat from * to end of round—8 sts.

Round 3: Knit.

Round 4: *KRL, K1, repeat from * to end of round—16 sts.

Round 5: Knit.

Round 6: *K1, M1L, K2, M1R, K1, repeat from * to end of round—24 sts.

Round 7: Knit.

Round 8: *K1, M1L, K4, M1R, K1, repeat from * to end of round—32 sts.

Round 9: Knit.

Round 10: *K1, M1L, K6, M1R, K1, repeat from * to end of round—40 sts.

Rounds 11–17: Knit.

Round 18: *SSK, K16, K2tog, repeat from * to end of round—36 sts.

Round 19: Knit.

Round 20: *SSK, K14, K2tog, repeat from * to end of round—32 sts.

Round 21: Knit.

Round 22: *SSK, K12, K2tog, repeat from * to end of round—28 sts.

Round 23: Knit.

Round 24: *SSK, K10, K2tog, repeat from * to end of round—24 sts.

Round 25: Knit.

Round 26: *SSK, K8, K2tog, repeat from * to end of round—20 sts.

Round 27: Knit.

If working with dpns, transfer half of sts to one needle. If working with two circular needles, half of sts will already be on one needle, making this step unnecessary. Either way, the next section is worked back and forth using just half the round of sts.

Shape the head by working short rows in the following manner:

Row 1: K9, w&t.

Row 2: P8, w&t.

Row 3: K1, M1R, K2, M1R, K2, M1L, K2, M1L, w&t.

Row 4: P10, w&t.

Row 5: K1, M1R, K3, M1R, K2, M1L, K3, M1L, w&t.

Row 6: P12, w&t.

Row 7: K1, M1R, K4, M1R, K2, M1L, K4, M1L, w&t.

Row 8: P14, w&t.

Row 9: K15, w&t.

Row 10: P16, w&t.

Row 11: K17, w&t

Row 12: P18, w&t.

Row 13: K5, SSK, K4, K2tog, K6, w&t.

Row 14: P18, w&t.

Complete the head by switching from short rows to rounds:

Round 28: K6, SSK, K2, K2tog, K7. Before working the first st, pick up a couple of the wraps from the junction between the short row section and the rest of the round. Knit these together with the next st (this is not an increase, just a measure to prevent holes from forming between the short row section and the rest of the round). K to end of round.

Round 29: Before working the first st, pick up a couple of the wraps from the junction between the short row section and the rest of the round. Knit these together with the first st. Continue as follows: K6, SSK, K2tog, K to end of round.

Round 30: K7, K2tog, K to end of round. BO all sts.

Arm Assembly

Pick up 3 sts in MC from the top selvedge of each arm for a total of 24 sts, as shown in **Figure 1**. Join in a round.

Figure 1

Rounds 1–3: Knit.

Round 4: K12, M1R, K12—25 sts.

BO all 25 sts.

Close the base of the arm assembly as follows. Turn the arm assembly upside down. In CC, pick up 40 sts from the underside of the arm assembly as shown in **Figure 2**.

Figure 2

Take extra care when picking up sts at the regions where the tentacles intersect, as holes can easily form in these areas. To prevent this, be sure to pick up 2 sts at each intersection point, one on each side of the middle st.

Join these 40 sts into a round and proceed in CC as follows:

Rounds 1–3: Knit.

Round 4: *K2tog, repeat from * to end of round—20 sts.

Round 5: Knit.

Round 6: *K2tog, repeat from * to end of round—10 sts.

Round 7: *K2tog, repeat from * to end—5 sts. Cut yarn and thread through remaining sts. Pull tight. The underside of your assembly should now resemble **Figure 3**.

Figure 3

Fold eight chenille stems in half and twist tightly. The folded chenille stems will have one blunt end (the folded end) and one sharp end. Carefully insert one folded chenille stem into each tentacle, blunt end first. When finished, all the sharp ends will be pointing toward the center of the assembly. Fold each chenille stem upward and twist all eight around each other as in **Figure 4**. Wrap with generous quantities of waste yarn until there are no more protruding sharp ends.

Figure 4

Finishing

Using bits of light and dark colored yarn, embroider eyes onto the head. Lightly stuff the head and mantle with fiberfill. Graft the tentacle assembly onto the head and mantle using fake grafting techniques. Weave in any loose ends with a tapestry needle.

Jellyfish

Jellyfish are beautiful, but potentially painful denizens of the sea. Luckily, this knit version is lovely, but lacks nematocysts. A relatively easy project, it will give you great practice with working simultaneously in multiple colors (stranded knitting), knitting in the round, and picking up stitches.

yarn
Worsted weight
MC (dusty rose): 30 yd (27.5 m)
Shown: Cascade 220 color #8834
CC1 (cement gray): 30 yd (27.5 m)
Shown: Cascade 220 color #8229
CC2 (pastel pink): 50 yd (46 m)
Shown: Cascade 220 color #4192

needles
· One set U.S. size 5 (3.75 mm) double-pointed needles
  and/or
· Two U.S. size 5 (3.75 mm) circular needles,
  24" (61 cm) long

notions
· Fiberfill stuffing
· Tapestry needle

gauge
22 to 24 sts = 4" (10 cm) in stockinette stitch

dimensions
Bell diameter: 4" (10 cm)
Oral arm length: 10" to 20"
(25.5 to 51 cm)

difficulty
Beginner/Intermediate

Pattern

Bell

In CC1, CO 4 sts. Join these sts into a round, and proceed:

Round 1: K-fb 4 times—8 sts.

Round 2: Knit.

Rounds 3-24: Follow chart. Note that for each round, you will be repeating the chart 8 times.

Chart

					20, 22, 24
K				Y	19, 21, 23
					18
K				Y	17
					16
K				Y	15
					14
K				Y	13
					12
					10
			Y		11
					8
		Y			9
		Y			7
					6
	Y				5
					4
Y					3

KEY

K = k2tog

Y = k1, m1l

Round 25: *K1, KLL, repeat from * to end of round—96 sts.

BO all sts as follows: *turn work and CO 3 sts using the cable CO method, BO 6 sts, repeat from * until all sts are bound off.

Underside of Bell

Turn work over. In MC, pick up 48 sts approximately 1" (2.5 cm) from the edge of the bell.

See **Figure 1** for guidance.

Figure 1

Join these sts into a round and continue:

Rounds 1-3: Knit.

Round 4: *K2tog, repeat from * to end of round—24 sts.

Round 5: Knit.

Round 6: *K2tog, repeat from * to end of round—12 sts.

Round 7: *K2tog, repeat from * to end of round—6 sts.

Stuff the bell with fiberfill. Do not overstuff! Cut yarn, thread through final 6 sts, and pull tight.

Oral Arms

You will be making 4 oral arms for your jelly.

To make the first arm, CO 35 sts in CC2 using the knit-on method. Continue, working back and forth in rows, as follows:

Row 1: [K-tbl, YO] 16 times, K-tbl 3 times, [YO, K-tbl] 16 times—67 sts.

Row 2: Sl1, K32, w&t.

Row 3: [K1, YO] 15 times, K-tbl 3 times, [YO, K1] 15 times—97 sts.

Row 4: Sl1, K30, w&t.

Row 5: [K1, YO] 30 times, K1—127 sts.
BO all sts. Cut yarn, thread through final lp, and pull tight.

To make the second arm, CO 51 sts in CC2 using the knit-on method. Continue, working back and forth in rows, as follows:

Row 1: [K-tbl, YO] 24 times, K-tbl 3 times, [YO, K-tbl] 24 times—99 sts.

Row 2: Sl1, K48, w&t.

Row 3: [K1, YO] 23 times, K-tbl 3 times, [YO, K1] 23 times—145 sts.

Row 4: Sl1, K46, w&t.

Row 5: [K1, YO] 46 times, K1—191 sts.

BO all sts. Cut yarn, thread through final lp, and pull tight.

To make the third oral arm, CO 65 sts in CC2 using the knit-on method. Continue, working back and forth in rows, as follows:

Row 1: [K-tbl, YO] 31 times, K-tbl 3 times, [YO, K-tbl] 31 times—127 sts.

Row 2: Sl1, K62, w&t.

Row 3: [K1, YO] 30 times, K-tbl 3 times, [YO, K1] 30 times—187 sts.

Row 4: Sl1, K60, w&t.

Row 5: [K1, YO] 60 times, K1—247 sts.

BO all sts. Cut yarn, thread through final lp, and pull tight.

To make the fourth oral arm, CO 99 sts in CC2 using the knit-on method. Continue, working back and forth in rows, as follows:

Row 1: [K-tbl, YO] 48 times, K-tbl 3 times, [YO, K-tbl] 48 times—195 sts.

Row 2: Sl1, K96, w&t.

Row 3: [K1, YO] 47 times, K-tbl 3 times, [YO, K1] 47 times—289 sts.

Row 4: Sl1, K94, w&t.

Row 5: [K1, YO] 94 times, K1—383 sts. BO all sts. Cut yarn, thread through final lp, and pull tight.

Stinging Tentacles

Cut a 9" and 15" (23 to 38 cm) length of CC1 yarn. Carefully separate the plies in each of these lengths to get several single-ply pieces. Attach these single-ply lengths to the edges of the bell.

Finishing

Attach the oral arms to the underside of the bell. Take care of any loose yarn ends.

Black-Devil Anglerfish

The mating behavior of the deep-sea angler fish is probably one of the most bizarre in the entire animal kingdom. Because locating a mate is a difficult affair in the sparsely populated deep ocean, a male who meets a female can't afford to let her get away. Being only one-tenth of her size, he attaches himself to her with his sharp teeth. Over time, his circulation fuses with hers, and he becomes a part of her, providing a lifetime supply of sperm for the pair's reproductive needs.

Depending on your tastes, you may knit this design with or without the parasitic male angler. Either way, this is a fun, quirky knit!

yarn
Worsted weight
MC (slate gray): 30 yd (27.5 m)
Shown: Cascade 220 color #9473
CC1 (gray lichen): 30 yd (27.5 m)
Shown: Cascade 220 color #7821
CC2 (navy): 25 yd (23 m)
Shown: Cascade 220 color #8393

needles
- One set U.S. size 5 (3.75 mm) double-pointed needles
and/or
- Two U.S. size 5 (3.75 mm) circular needles, 24" (61 cm) long
- Stitch holder

notions
- Fiberfill stuffing
- Tapestry needle
- One 12" (30.5 cm) chenille stem (optional)

gauge
22 to 24 sts = 4" (10 cm) in stockinette stitch

dimensions
Length: 8" (20 cm)
Height: 4" (10 cm)

difficulty
Intermediate/
Experienced

Pattern

Dorsum (Upper Side)

In MC, CO 8 sts. Continue, working back and forth in rows:

Row 1: Sl1, P6, K1.

Row 2: Sl1, K2, M1R, K2, M1L, K3—10 sts.

Row 3: Sl1, P8, K1.

Row 4: Sl1, K3, M1R, K2, M1L, K4—12 sts.

Row 5: Sl1, P10, K1.

Row 6: Sl1, K4, M1R, K2, M1L, K5—14 sts.

Row 7: Sl1, P12, K1.

Row 8: Sl1, K5, M1R, K2, M1L, K6—16 sts.

Row 9: Sl1, P14, K1.

Row 10: Sl1, K6, M1R, K2, M1L, K7—18 sts.

Row 11: Sl1, P16, K1.

Row 12: Sl1, K7, M1R, K2, M1L, K8—20 sts.

Row 13: Sl1, P18, K1.

Row 14: Sl1, K8, M1R, K2, M1L, K9—22 sts.

Row 15: Sl1, P20, K1.

Row 16: Sl1, K9, M1R, K2, M1L, K10—24 sts.

Row 17: Sl1, P22, K1.

Row 18: Sl1, K10, M1R, K2, M1L, K11—26 sts.

Row 19: Sl1, P24, K1.

Row 20: Sl1, K11, M1R, K2, M1L, K12—28 sts.

Row 21: Sl1, P26, K1.

Row 22: Sl1, K12, M1R, K2, M1L, K13—30 sts.

Row 23: Sl1, P28, K1.

Row 24: Sl1, K13, M1R, K2, M1L, K14—32 sts.

Row 25: Sl1, P30, K1.

Row 26: Sl1, K14, M1R, K2, M1L, K15—34 sts.

Row 27: Sl1, P32, K1.

Row 28: Sl1, K15, M1R, K2, M1L, K16—36 sts.

Row 29: Sl1, P34, K1.

Row 30: Sl1, K16, M1R, K2, M1L, K17—38 sts.

Row 31: Sl1, P36, K1.

Row 32: Sl1, K17, M1R, K2, M1L, K18—40 sts.

Row 33: Sl1, P38, K1.

Row 34: Sl1, K27, w&t.

Row 35: P16, w&t.

Row 36: K3, SSK, K6, K2tog, K7, w&t—38 sts.

Row 37: P22, w&t.

Row 38: K7, SSK, K4, K2tog, K11, w&t—36 sts.

Row 39: P28, w&t.

Row 40: K11, SSK, K2, K2tog, K15, w&t—34 sts.

Row 41: Sl1, P32, K1.

BO all sts.

Belly (Lower Side)

Use MC yarn and pick up 28 sts kwise along the selvedge of the work, beginning at the tail region and moving toward the head. Continue working in rows as follows:

Row 1: P10, w&t.

Row 2: K6, [M1R, K1] 3 times, P1—31 sts.

Row 3: Sl1, P15, w&t.

Row 4: K9, [K1, M1R, K1] 3 times, P1—34 sts.

Row 5: Sl1, P21, w&t.

Row 6: K12, [K2, M1R, K1] 3 times, P1—37 sts.

Row 7: Sl1, P27, w&t.

Row 8: K15, [K3, M1R, K1] 3 times, P1—40 sts.

Row 9: Sl1, P33, w&t.

Row 10: K18, [K4, M1R, K1] 3 times, P1—43 sts.

Row 11: Sl1, P39, w&t.

Row 12: K21, [K5, M1R, K1] 3 times, P1—46 sts.

Row 13: Sl1, P45.

Row 14: K24, [K6, M1R, K1] 3 times, P1—49 sts.

Row 15: Sl1, P48.

Cut MC yarn, and place 49 sts on a holder. Turn work, and pick up another 28 sts kwise from the opposite selvedge of the work, beginning at the head region and traveling toward the tail. Continue working in rows as follows:

Row 1: P28.

Row 2: Sl1, [K1, M1L] 3 times, K6, w&t—31 sts.

Row 3: P13.

Row 4: Sl1, [K1, M1L, K1] 3 times, K9, w&t—34 sts.

Row 5: P19.

Row 6: Sl1, [K1, M1L, K2] 3 times, K12, w&t—37 sts.

Row 7: P25.

Row 8: Sl1, [K1, M1L, K3] 3 times, K15, w&t—40 sts.

Row 9: P31.

Row 10: Sl1, [K1, M1L, K4] 3 times, K18, w&t—43 sts.

Row 11: P37.

Row 12: Sl1, [K1, M1L, K5] 3 times, K21, w&t—46 sts.

Row 13: P43.

Row 14: Sl1, [K1, M1L, K6] 3 times, K23, P1—49 sts.

Row 15: Sl1, P48.

Row 16: Sl1, K47, P1.

Row 17: Sl1, P48.

Cut MC yarn, leaving a long tail. Using this long yarn tail and a tapestry needle, graft (Kitchener stitch) the 49 sts from the first needle to the 49 sts on the second needle.

Upper Lip

Using CC1, pick up 34 sts from the BO edge of the dorsum. Work these sts as follows:

Row 1: P33, K1.

Row 2: Sl1, K33.

Row 3: Sl1, P32, K1.

Row 4: Sl1, K33.

Row 5: Sl1, P29, w&t.

Row 6: K26, w&t.

Row 7: P22, w&t.

Row 8: K18, w&t.

Row 9: P25, K1.

BO all sts. Cut CC1 yarn, leaving a long tail. Using long tail of yarn and a tapestry needle, fold the lip up and whip st the BO edge to the upper edge where you picked up the sts initially.

Lower Lip

Using CC1, pick up 30 sts from the selvedge on the bottom of the jaw. Continue working these sts as follows:

Row 1: Sl1, P28, K1.

Row 2: Sl1, K29.

Row 3: Sl1, P28, K1.

Row 4: Sl1, K29.

Row 5: Sl1, P25, w&t.

Row 6: K10, M1R, K2, M1L, K10, w&t.

Row 7: P20, w&t.

Row 8: K7, M1R, K2, M1L, K7, w&t.

Row 9: P14, w&t.

Row 10: K10, w&t.

Row 11: P16, w&t.

Row 12: K9, K2tog, SSK, K9, w&t.

Row 13: P25, K1.

Row 14: Sl1, K12, K2tog, SSK, K13.

BO all sts. Cut CC1 yarn, leaving a long tail. Using this long yarn tail, whip st the BO edge of the lower lip to the edge of the chin where you originally picked up sts.

Inside of Mouth

Using **Figure 1** as a guide, pick up a total of 27 sts in CC2 yarn on the inside edge of the lower lip.

Figure 1

Continue, working in rows, as follows:

Row 1: Sl1, P24, w&t.

Row 2: K23, w&t.

Row 3: P21, w&t.

Row 4: K19, w&t.

Row 5: P17, w&t.

Row 6: K15, w&t.

Row 7: P14, w&t.

Row 8: K13, w&t.

Row 9: P15, w&t.

Row 10: K17, w&t.

Row 11: P19, w&t.

Row 12: K21, w&t.

Row 13: P23, K1.

Row 14: Sl1, K26.

BO all sts.

Stuff the body of the fish with fiberfill, being careful not to overstuff.

Cut CC3 yarn, leaving a long tail. Using a tapestry needle and this long tail, whip st this BO edge to the inner edge of the upper lip.

Tail Fin

Use MC yarn, and beginning from the midline of the back, pick up 10 sts along the open end of the tail region. Turn the work, and pick up an additional 10 sts along the other side of the opening for a total of 20 sts. Use **Figure 2** as a guide to the placement of these sts.

Figure 2

Join these sts into a round and continue:

Rounds 1 & 2: Knit.

Round 3: [K1, M1L, K3, M1R, K1] 4 times—28 sts.

Cut MC yarn, and switch to CC1. Continue:

Rounds 4-9: [K1, P1, K1, P1, K1, P1, K1] 4 times.

Round 10: [SSK, K1, P1, K1, P1, K2, P1, K1, P1, K1, K2tog] 2 times—24 sts.

Round 11: [K2, P1, K1, P1, K2, P1, K1, P1, K2] 2 times.

Round 12: [SSK, P1, K1, P1, K2, P1, K1, P1, K2tog] 2 times—20 sts.

Round 13: [K1, P1, K1, P1, K1] 4 times.

Cut yarn, leaving a long tail. Divide the 20 sts evenly between two needles. Using your tapestry needle, graft (Kitchener st) the sts on the first needle to the sts on the second needle.

Dorsal Fin

Using CC1 yarn, pick up 15 sts along the midline of the back near the tail fin. When picking up these sts, begin at the tail region and continue along the midline of the back toward the head region. Turn the work, and, using a new needle, pick up another 15 sts directly behind the first 15 sts. Use **Figure 3** as a guide to the placement of these sts.

Figure 3

Join these 30 sts into a round and continue:

Round 1: *[K1, P1] 7 times, K1, repeat from * to end of round.

Round 2: SSK, [K1, P1] 6 times, K2, [P1, K1] 6 times, K2tog—28 sts.

Round 3: SSK, [P1, K1] 6 times, [K1, P1] 6 times, K2tog—26 sts.

Round 4: SSK, [K1, P1] 5 times, K2, [P1, K1] 5 times, K2tog—24 sts.

Round 5: SSK, [P1, K1] 5 times, [K1, P1] 5 times, K2tog—22 sts.

Round 6: SSK, [K1, P1] 3 times, K1, K2tog, SSK, K1, [P1, K1] 3 times, K2tog—18 sts.

Cut yarn, leaving a long tail. Divide 18 sts evenly onto two needles and, using a tapestry needle, graft (Kitchener st) the sts from the first needle to the sts on the second needle.

Pectoral Fins

Using MC yarn, pick up 6 sts along the side of the body. Turn work and pick up another 6 sts directly behind the first 6 sts. Use **Figure 4** as a guide to the placement of these sts.

Figure 4

Join these 12 sts into a round and continue:

Rounds 1 & 2: Knit.

Round 3: [K1, M1L, K1, M1R, K1] 4 times—20 sts.

Cut MC yarn, and attach CC1 yarn. Continue:

Rounds 4-8: [K1, P1, K1, P1, K1] 4 times.

Round 9: *SSK, [K1, P1, K1] 2 times, K2tog, repeat from * to end of round—16 sts.

Round 10: [K2, P1, K2, P1, K2] 2 times.

Round 11: [SSK, P1, K2, P1, K2tog] 2 times—12 sts.

Round 12: [K1, P1, K1] 4 times.

Cut yarn, leaving a long tail. Divide 12 sts evenly onto two needles. Using a tapestry needle, graft (Kitchener st) the sts from the first needle to the sts on the second needle.

Work the opposite pectoral fin by picking up 12 sts on the opposite side of the body and working identically.

Teeth *(Make 4)*

In CC3, CO 4 sts. Work seven rows of I-cord. Work three more rows as follows, continuing to work as I-cord:

Row 1: K2tog, K2.

Row 2: K3.

Row 3: K2tog, K1.

Cut yarn, thread through remaining two sts, and pull tight.

Lure

In MC, CO 30 sts. Continue, working back and forth in rows:

Row 1: Sl1, P29.

Row 2: Sl1, K4, w&t.

Row 3: P5.

Row 4: Sl1, K28, P1.

Row 5: Sl1, P3, w&t.

Row 6: K3, P1.

Row 7: Sl1, P29.

Row 8: Sl1, K4, w&t.

Row 9: P5.

Row 10: Sl1, K28, P1.

Continuing with MC yarn, turn the work, and using a second needle, pick up another 30 sts from the CO edge of the work. Cut MC yarn, leaving a long tail. Using this long yarn tail and a tapestry needle, graft (Kitchener st) the 30 sts on the original needle to the 30 sts on the second needle.

Now, use CC1 to pick up 8 sts around the circumference of the smaller end of the tube.

Join these 8 sts in a round and continue:

Rounds 1–2: Knit.

Cut CC1 yarn, and attach CC3 to work. Continue:

Round 3: [K1, KLL, KRL, K1] 4 times—16 sts.

Round 4: Knit.

Round 5: [K1, M1L, K2, M1R, K1] 4 times—24 sts.

Rounds 6–8: Knit.

Round 9: [SSK, K8, K2tog] 2 times—20 sts.

Round 10: Knit.

Round 11: [SSK, K6, K2tog] 2 times—16 sts.

Round 12: Knit.

Round 13: [SSK, K4, K2tog] 2 times—12 sts.

Round 14: [SSK, K2, K2tog] 2 times—8 sts.

Cut CC3 yarn, leaving a long tail. Stuff the tip of the lure with fiberfill.

Divide remaining 8 sts evenly onto two needles. Using long yarn tail and tapestry needle, graft (Kitchener st) the sts on the first needle to the sts on the second needle.

Parasitic Male *(Optional)*

You may position the parasitic male anywhere on the body of the female angler. Use MC to pick up 4 sts in desired location. Turn the work and pick up another 4 sts behind the first 4 sts. Join these 8 sts into a round and continue:

Round 1: Knit.

Round 2: [K1, M1L, K2, M1L, K1] 2 times –12 sts.

Rounds 3–7: Knit.

Round 8: [SSK, K2, K2tog] 2 times—8 sts.

Stuff the body of the male with fiberfill. Continue:

Round 9: [SSK, K2tog] 2 times—4 sts.

Round 10: Knit.

Round 11: [K1, KLL, KRL, K1] 2 times—8 sts.

Switch to CC1 and continue.

Rounds 12: [K1, P2, K1] 2 times.

Round 13: [K1, P1, KLL, KRL, P1, K1] 2 times— 12 sts.

Rounds 14–15: [K1, P1, K1] 4 times.

Cut yarn, leaving a long tail. Divide 12 sts evenly onto two needles. Using long yarn tail, graft (Kitchener st) the sts on the first needle to the sts on the second needle.

Finishing

If desired, fold a chenille stem in half, tightly twist it, and insert it into the lure. Attach (mattress st) the lure to the midline of the forehead. Use CC3 yarn to embroider eyes onto the head of the angler. Embroider eyes onto the parasitic male (if applicable). Attach the four teeth to the inside of the mouth.

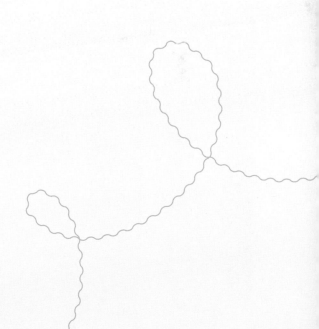

Sea Star

This lovely little echinoderm is quick and easy, a great knit for those times when you're seeking some instant gratification. It will also help you practice decreases, short rows, and picking up stitches. Make an entire collection in varying yarn weights and colors for a real plush treat!

yarn

Worsted weight
MC indigo/lapis): 40 yd (36.5 m)
Shown: Cascade 220 Paints color #9930
CC (taupe): 40 yd (36.5 m)
Shown: Cascade 220 color #8021

needles

• One set U.S. size 5 (3.75 mm) double-pointed needles
and/or
• Two U.S. size 5 (3.75 mm) circular needles,
24" (61 cm) long

notions

• Fiberfill stuffing
• Tapestry needle

gauge

22 to 24 sts = 4" (10 cm) in stockinette stitch

dimensions

Diameter: 8" (20 cm)

difficulty

Beginner/Intermediate

Pattern

Arms *(Make 5)*

In MC, CO 15 sts. Continue working back and forth in rows as follows:

Row 1: Sl1, P13, K1.

Row 2: Sl1, K5, Sl2-K1-P2SSO, K6—13 sts.

Rows 3 & 5: Sl1, P11, K1.

Row 4: Sl1, K12.

Row 6: Sl1, K4, Sl2-K1-P2SSO, K5—11 sts.

Rows 7 & 9: Sl1, P9, K1.

Row 8: Sl1, K10.

Row 10: Sl1, K3, Sl2-K1-P2SSO, K4—9 sts.

Rows 11 & 13: Sl1, P7, K1.

Row 12: Sl1, K8.

Row 14: Sl1, K2, Sl2-K1-P2SSO, K3—7 sts.

Rows 15 & 17: Sl1, P5, K1.

Row 16: Sl1, K6.

Row 18: Sl1, K1, Sl2-K1-P2SSO, K2—5 sts.

Rows 19 & 21: Sl1, P3, K1.

Row 20: Sl1, K4.

Row 22: Sl1, Sl2-K1-P2SSO, K1—3 sts.

Row 23: Sl2-P1-P2SSO—1 st.

Cut yarn, thread through final st and pull tight. Beginning from the base of the arm and ending at the tip, use CC and pick up 12 sts from the selvedge of the arm. You will be picking these sts up kwise from the right side of the work at a rate of 1 st per two rows. Turn the work. Beginning at the tip and ending at the base of the arm, pick up another 12 sts from the other selvedge of the arm. Once again, you will be picking these sts up kwise from the right side of the work at a rate of 1 st per two rows. See **Figure 1** for guidance. You should now have a total of 24 sts.

Figure 1

Continue, working back and forth in rows, as follows:

Row 1 (wrong side): Sl1, K7, w&t.

Row 2: P8.

Row 3: Sl1, K3, w&t.

Row 4: P4.

Row 5: Sl1, K10, P2tog-tbls, P2tog, K10, P1—24 sts.

Row 6: Sl1, P5, w&t.

Row 7: K5, P1.

Row 8: Sl1, P9, K1.

Divide 24 sts evenly onto two needles. Using the three-needle BO method, BO all sts. Cut yarn, thread through final st and pull tight.

Assembly of Arms

In MC, pick up 8 sts from the CO edge of each of the five arms for a total of 40 sts. See **Figure 2** for guidance.

Join these sts into a round and proceed:

Round 1: Knit.

Round 2: *K6, K2tog, repeat from * to end of round—35 sts.

Round 3: *K5, K2tog, repeat from * to end of round—30 sts.

Round 4: *K4, K2tog, repeat from * to end of round—25 sts.

Round 5: *K3, K2tog, repeat from * to end of round—20 sts.

Round 6: *K2, K2tog, repeat from * to end of round—15 sts.

Round 7: *K1, K2tog, repeat from * to end of round—10 sts.

Round 8: *K2tog, repeat from * to end of round—5 sts.

Cut yarn, thread through final 5 sts and pull tight.

Figure 2

Underside

Turn the work over. Using CC yarn, pick up a total of 70 sts around the open underside of the sea star. Pick up these sts as follows: 6 sts in between each of the arms and 8 sts on the CC selvedge of the underside of each arm. See **Figure 3** for guidance in picking up these sts. Join these 70 sts into a round and continue:

Figure 3

Rounds 1–3: Knit.

Round 4: *K2tog 17 times, K1, repeat from * to end of round—36 sts.

Round 5: Knit.

Round 6: *K2tog, repeat from * to end of round—18 sts.
Carefully stuff the arms of the sea star and the central body region with fiberfill. Do not overstuff! Continue:

Round 7: *K2tog 4 times, K1, repeat from * to end of round—10 sts.

Round 8: *K2tog 2 times, K1, repeat from * to end of round—6 sts.

Cut yarn, thread through final 6 sts and pull tight.

Finishing

Take care of any loose yarn ends.

Sun Star

Sun stars are among the most voracious invertebrate predators, which is one reason that many undersea enthusiasts don't include them in home aquariums. This knit sun star, on the other hand, will make a lovely addition to your undersea collection, and you don't need to worry about its appetite at all! It also provides great practice with short rows, picking up stitches, and knitting in the round.

yarn

Worsted weight
MC (dark orange): 60 yd (55 m)
Shown: Cascade 220 color #9465B
CC (yellow): 30 yd (27.5 m)
Shown: Cascade 220 color #4147

needles

· One set U.S. size 5 (3.75 mm) double-pointed needles
and/or
· Two U.S. size 5 (3.75 mm) circular needles, 24" (61 cm) long

notions

· Fiberfill stuffing
· Tapestry needle

gauge

22 to 24 sts = 4" (10 cm) in stockinette stitch

dimensions

Diameter: 10" (25.5 cm)

difficulty

Beginner/Intermediate

Pattern

Arms *(Make 12)*

CO 24 sts in CC. Change to MC and continue:

Row 1: Sl1, P23.

Row 2: Sl1, K11, w&t.

Row 3: P12.

Row 4: Sl1, K2, w&t.

Row 5: P3.

Row 6: Sl1, K14, w&t.

Row 7: P15.

Row 8: Sl1, K5, w&t.

Row 9: P6.

Row 10: Sl1, K17, w&t.

Row 11: P18.

Row 12: Sl1, K8, w&t.

Row 13: P9.

Row 14: Sl1, K20, w&t.

Row 15: P21.

Row 16: Sl1, K23.

Cut MC yarn, leaving a long tail and reattach CC. Continue:

Row 17: Sl1, P23.

BO all sts. Cut CC yarn, leaving a long tail. Using a tapestry needle and long yarn tail, whip st the CO edge to the BO edge.

Leave all the yarn tails long and use them to stuff the center as you close the underside later.

Assembly of Arms

Use MC, and pick up 4 sts from the upper selvedge of each arm, for a total of 48 sts. See **Figure 1** for guidance.

Figure 1

Join these sts into a round and continue:

Round 1: Knit.

Round 2: *K2, K2tog, repeat from * to end of round—36 sts.

Round 3: Knit.

Round 4: *K1, K2tog, repeat from * to end of round—24 sts.

Round 5: Knit.

Round 6: *K2tog, repeat from * to end of round—12 sts.

Round 7: Knit.

Round 8: *K2tog, repeat from * to end of round—6 sts.

Cut MC yarn, thread through final 6 sts, and pull tight.

Closing the Underside

Using **Figure 2** as a guide, pick up 60 sts in CC from the perimeter of the underside opening.

Figure 2

Join these sts into a round and continue.

Rounds 1–3: Knit.

Round 4: *K2tog, repeat from * to end of round—30 sts.

Round 5 & 6: Knit.

Round 7: *K2tog, repeat from * to end of round—15 sts.

Round 8: Knit.

Round 9: K2tog 3 times, K1, K2tog 4 times—8 sts.

Round 10: *K2tog, repeat from * to end of round—4 sts.

Cut yarn, thread through final 4 sts, and pull tight.

Finishing

Take care of any loose yarn ends. Enjoy your little echinoderm!

Garden Variety:
backyard critters

Grab a magnifying glass and step into the closest patch of nature. You'll be amazed by the variety of what you'll find. Knit up some of these garden amigurumi creatures and pay homage to the tiniest, but most important, residents of our natural ecosystems.

Earthworm

These burrowing little guys are the most important critters in any garden. They are the original tillers of the soil, working silently underfoot to make lovely greenery grow above. This knit version is a relatively quick knit and will give you great practice in working with short rows, picking up stitches, and Kitchener stitch. Because the body is worked in ribbing, which tends to knit up loosely, you may have to use smaller needles than you normally would to achieve a tight enough gauge.

yarn

Worsted weight
MC (sweet mauve): 50 yd (46 m)
Shown: Cascade 220 color #8114
CC (dusty rose): 20 yd (18 m)
Shown: Cascade 220 color #8834

needles

· One set U.S. size 5 (3.75 mm) double-pointed needles
and/or
· Two U.S. size 5 (3.75 mm) circular needles,
 24" (61 cm) long

notions

· Fiberfill stuffing
· Tapestry needle

gauge

22 to 24 sts = 4" (10 cm) in stockinette stitch

dimensions

Length: 10" (25.5 cm)

difficulty

Beginner/Intermediate

Pattern

Body

In MC, CO 71 sts. Continue, working back and forth in rows:

Row 1 (wrong side): Sl1, [P1, K1] 35 times.

Row 2: Sl1, [K1, P1] 33 times, K1, w&t.

Row 3: [P1, K1] 32 times, P1, w&t.

Row 4: [K1, P1] 31 times, K1, w&t.

Row 5: [P1, K1] 30 times, P1, w&t.

Row 6: [K1, P1] 29 times, K1, w&t.

Row 7: [P1, K1] 28 times, P1, w&t.

Row 8: [K1, P1] 27 times, K1, w&t.

Row 9: [P1, K1] 31 times.

Row 10: Sl1, [K1, P1] 34 times, K2.

Continuing with MC yarn, use a new needle to pick up 71 sts along the CO edge of the work. Cut yarn, leaving a long tail. Using a tapestry needle and long yarn tail, graft (Kitchener st) the 71 sts from the first needle to the 71 sts on the second needle. While grafting, gently stuff the body of the worm with fiberfill. Do not overstuff!

Cuff (Clitellum)

In CC yarn, CO 15 sts. Continue, working back and forth in rows:

Rows 1, 3, 5, 7, 9, 11, 13, 15, 17: Sl1, P14.

Rows 2, 4, 6, 8, 10, 12, 14, 16, 18: Sl1, K13, P1.

Continuing with CC, use a new needle and pick up 15 sts along the CO edge of the work. Cut yarn, leaving a long tail. Using a tapestry needle and this long yarn tail, graft (Kitchener st) the 15 sts from the first needle to the 15 sts on the second needle.

Finishing

Place the cuff on the body of the worm. If desired, sew the cuff onto the body. Take care of any loose yarn ends. Enjoy your new friend!

Praying Mantis

It's always a real treat to find these gorgeous gals in the garden! In addition to be being absolutely lovely to behold, they are also highly adept predators, controlling pest species to maintain a balanced backyard environment. This knit version is huge, on both scale and charm. It's an involved knit, though well worth the effort. Have fun with the colors, as mantises come in a variety of beautiful shades!

yarn

Worsted weight
MC (spring shoot green): 100 yd (91 m)
Shown: Cascade 220 color #8903
CC (sweet lavender): 45 yd (41 m)
Shown: Cascade 220 color #8912

needles

• One set U.S. size 5 (3.75 mm) double-pointed needles
and/or
• Two U.S. size 5 (3.75 mm) circular needles, 24" (61 cm) long

notions

• Fiberfill stuffing
• Tapestry needle
• Six 12" (30.5 cm) chenille stems (optional)

gauge

22 to 24 sts = 4" (10 cm) in stockinette stitch

dimensions

Length (from top of head to tip of abdomen): 15" (38 cm)

difficulty

Experienced

Pattern

Abdomen and Thorax

In MC, CO 4 sts. Continue working back and forth in rows as follows:

Row 1: Sl1, P3.

Row 2: Sl1, M1R, K2, M1L, P1—6 sts.

Row 3: Sl1, P5.

Row 4: Sl1, K1, M1R, K2, M1L, K1, P1—8 sts.

Row 5: Sl1, P7.

Row 6: Sl1, K2, M1R, K2, M1L, K2, P1—10 sts.

Row 7: Sl1, P9.

Row 8: Sl1, K3, M1R, K2, M1L, K3, P1—12 sts.

Row 9: Sl1, P11.

Row 10: Sl1, K4, M1R, K2, M1L, K4, P1—14 sts.

Row 11: Sl1, P13.

Row 12: Sl1, K5, M1R, K2, M1L, K5, P1—16 sts.

Row 13: Sl1, P15.

Row 14: Sl1, K6, M1R, K2, M1L, K6, P1—18 sts.

Row 15: Sl1, P17.

Row 16: Sl1, K7, M1R, K2, M1L, K7, P1—20 sts.

Row 17: Sl1, P19.

Row 18: Sl1, SSK, K6, M1R, K2, M1L, K6, K2tog, P1.

Row 19: Sl1, P19.

Rows 20-29: Repeat rows 18 & 19 five more times.

Row 30: Sl1, SSK, K3, w&t—19 sts.

Row 31: P5.

Row 32: Sl1, SSK, K5, M1R, K2, M1L, K6, K2tog, P1.

Row 33: Sl1, P5, w&t.

Row 34: K3, K2tog, P1—18 sts.

Row 35: Sl1, P17.

Row 36: Sl1, SSK, K5, M1R, K2, M1L, K5, K2tog, P1.

Row 37: Sl1, P5, w&t.

Row 38: K3, K2tog, P1—17 sts.

Row 39: Sl1, P16.

Row 40: Sl1, SSK, K3, w&t—16 sts.

Row 41: P5.

Row 42: Sl1, SSK, K4, M1R, K2, M1L, K4, K2tog, P1.

Row 43: Sl1, P4, w&t.

Row 44: K2, K2tog, P1—15 sts.

Row 45: Sl1, P14.

Row 46: Sl1, SSK, K2, w&t—14 sts.

Row 47: P4.

Row 48: Sl1, SSK, K3, M1R, K2, M1L, K3, K2tog, P1.

Row 49: Sl1, P3, w&t.

Row 50: K1, K2tog, P1—13 sts.

Row 51: Sl1, P12.

Row 52: Sl1, SSK, K1, w&t—12 sts.

Row 53: P3.

Row 54: Sl1, SSK, K2, M1R, K2, M1L, K2, K2tog, P1.

Row 55: Sl1, P1, K3, P2, K3, P2.

Row 56: Sl1, SSK, K2, M1R, K2, M1L, K2, K2tog, P1.

Row 57: Sl1, P11.

Rows 58-81: Repeat rows 56 & 57 twelve more times.

Row 82: Repeat row 56.

Row 83: Sl1, P2tog, P6, P2tog-tbl, P1—10 sts.

Row 84: Sl1, SSK, K1, M1R, K2, M1L, K1, K2tog, P1.

Row 85: Sl1, P2tog, P4, P2tog-tbl, P1—8 sts.

Row 86: Sl1, SSK, M1R, K2, M1L, K2tog, P1.

Row 87: Sl1, P2tog, P2, P2tog-tbl, P1—6 sts.

Row 88: Sl1, SSK, K2tog, P1—4 sts.
BO all sts.

Grabbing Legs *(Make 2)*

In MC, CO 10 sts. Continue, working back and forth in rows:

Row 1: Sl1, P9.

Row 2: Sl1, SSK, K1, M1R, K2, M1L, K1, K2tog, P1.

Rows 3-22: Repeat rows 1 & 2 ten more times.

Row 23: Sl1, P2tog, P4, P2tog-tbl, P1—8 sts.

Row 24: Sl1, SSK, M1R, K2, M1L, K2tog, P1.

Row 25: Sl1, P7.

Row 26: Repeat row 24.

Row 27: Sl1, P2tog, P2, P2tog-tbl, P1—6 sts.

Row 28: Sl1, K1, w&t.

Row 29: P2.

Row 30: Sl1, K4, P1.

Row 31: Sl1, P1, w&t.

Row 32: K1, P1.

Row 33: Sl, P5.

Rows 34-45: Repeat rows 28-33 two more times.

Row 46: Sl1, K1, M1R, K2, M1L, K1, P1—8 sts.

Row 47: Sl1, P7.

Row 48: Sl1, K2, M1R, K2, M1L, K2, P1—10 sts.

Row 49: Sl1, P9.

Row 50: Sl1, SSK, K1, M1R, K2, M1L, K1, K2tog, P1.

Rows 51–58: Repeat rows 49 & 50 four more times.

Row 59: Sl1, P2tog, P4, P2tog-tbl, P1—8 sts.

Row 60: Sl1, SSK, M1R, K2, M1L, K2tog, P1.

Row 61: Sl1, P7.

Row 62: Repeat row 60.

Row 63: Sl1, P2tog, P2, P2tog-tbl, P1—6 sts.

Row 64: Sl1, K3, w&t.

Row 65: P2, w&t.

Row 66: K3, P1.

Row 67: Sl1, P5.

Rows 68–71: Repeat rows 64–67.

Row 72: Sl1, K1, M1R, K2, M1L, K1, P1—8 sts.

Row 73: Sl1, P7.

Row 74: Sl1, K2, M1R, K2, M1L, K2, P1—10 sts.

Row 75: Sl1, P9.

Row 76: Sl1, SSK, K1, M1R, K2, M1L, K1, K2tog, P1.

Row 77 & 78: Repeat rows 75 & 76.

Row 79: Sl1, P2tog, P4, P2tog-tbl, P1—8 sts.

Row 80: Sl1, SSK, M1R, K2, M1L, K2tog, P1.

Row 81: Sl1, P7.

Row 82: Repeat row 80.

Row 83: Sl1, P2tog, P2, P2tog-tbl, P1—6 sts.

Row 84: Sl1, SSK, K2tog, K1—4 sts.

Work the following rows as I-cord, by sliding sts to opposite end of needle after each row.

Rows 85–88: Knit.

Row 89: K1, K2tog, K1—3 sts.

Row 90: Knit.

Row 91: K2tog, K1—2 sts.

Row 92: K2tog—1 st.

Cut yarn, thread through remaining st, and pull tight.

Using CC, pick up 58 sts kwise from one selvedge of the grasping leg, moving from the base to the tip. Turn the work and, using a second needle, pick up another 58 sts kwise from the opposite selvedge of the same leg, moving from the underside of the tip to the base. See **Figure 1** for guidance.

Figure 1

Cut CC yarn, leaving a long tail. Using a tapestry needle and this long yarn tail, graft the 58 sts from the first needle to the 58 sts from the second needle. While grafting, stuff the grasping leg with fiberfill. Do not overstuff. If you desire a pose-able leg, nestle a chenille stem along the length of the grasping leg and stuff fiberfill around it.

Legs *(Make 4)*

Use MC and CO 57 sts. Continue, working back and forth in rows:

Row 1: Sl1, P5, w&t.

Row 2: K4, w&t.

Row 3: P24, w&t.

Row 4: K18, w&t.

Row 5: P38, w&t.

Row 6: K18, w&t.

Row 7: P29.

Row 8: Sl1, K8, w&t.

Row 9: P9.

Row 10: Sl1, K56.

BO all sts. Cut MC yarn, leaving a long tail. Using a tapestry needle and this long yarn tail, whip stitch the CO edge to the BO edge.

Thorax and Abdomen Assembly

First, using **Figure 2** as a guide, sew (mattress stitch) the grasping legs to the inside of the thorax. You will be sewing each grasping leg to opposite selvedges of the thorax region.

Figure 2

Now, use **Figure 3** as a guide to pick up 24 sts in MC around the opening of the neck hole. You will be picking up the sts as follows: 5 sts from the CO edge of the left grasping leg, 7 sts from the left selvedge of the thorax, 7 sts from the right selvedge of the thorax, and 5 sts from the CO edge of the right grasping leg.

Figure 3

Cut yarn, leaving a long tail. Divide sts evenly onto two needles by placing the first 12 sts on one needle, and the second 12 sts on a second needle. Using tapestry needle and this long yarn tail, graft the sts from the first needle to the sts from the second needle. While grafting, gently stuff the neck region with fiberfill. Next, sew the four back legs to the inner selvedge near the base of the thoracic region (denoted by the row of purl sts separating the abdomen from the thorax). Use **Figure 4** as a guide. Note that you will be sewing 2 legs to the left side of the thorax base and 2 legs to the right side of the thorax base.

Figure 4

Now, use **Figure 5** to pick up sts around the mid-thoracic opening as follows: 2 sts along the upper face of the left hind leg, 10 sts along the left selvedge of the thorax, 4 sts along the underside of the left grasping leg, 4 sts along the underside of the right grasping leg, 10 sts along the right selvedge of the thorax, and 2 sts along the upper face of the right hind leg.

Figure 5

Join these 32 sts into a round. Knit one round. Cut yarn, leaving a long tail. Divide sts evenly onto two needles by placing the first 16 sts onto one needle and the second 16 sts onto a second needle. Using tapestry needle and this long yarn tail, graft (Kitchener st) the sts from the first needle to the sts on the second needle.

While grafting, stuff the thorax with fiberfill. If desired, insert chenille stems into the hind legs. Next, use **Figure 6** as a guide to sew edges of the four hind legs together.

Figure 6

Finally, use CC to pick up sts from one side of the open underside of the abdomen as follows: 36 sts from the left selvedge of the abdomen and 2 sts from the underside of the left rear leg. Use **Figure 7** as a guide in picking up these sts.

Figure 7

Continue, working back and forth along these 38 sts:

Row 1: Sl1, P34, w&t.

Row 2: K33, w&t.

Row 3: P30, w&t.

Row 4: K28, w&t.

Row 5: P25, w&t.

Row 6: K23, w&t.

Row 7: P20, w&t.

Row 8: K18, w&t.

Row 9: P15, w&t.

Row 10: K13, w&t.

Row 11: P15, w&t.

Row 12: K16, w&t.

Row 13: P19, w&t.

Row 14: K21, w&t.

Row 15: P24, w&t.

Row 16: K26, w&t.

Row 17: P29, w&t.

Row 18: K31, w&t.

Row 19: P34, K1.

Row 20: Sl1, K37.

Continue with CC yarn and, using a second needle, pick up another 38 sts on the opposite selvedge of the abdominal opening as follows: 2 sts from the underside of the right rear leg, and 36 sts from the right selvedge of the abdomen. Use **Figure 8** as a guide in picking up these sts.

Figure 8

Cut yarn, leaving a long tail. Using a tapestry needle and this long yarn tail, graft (Kitchener st) the 38 sts from the first needle to the 38 sts from the second needle. While grafting, stuff the abdominal region with fiberfill. Do not overstuff.

Head

In MC, CO 12 sts. Continue, working back and forth in rows:

Row 1: Sl1, P9, w&t.

Row 2: K8, w&t.

Row 3: P7, w&t.

Row 4: K6, w&t.

Row 5: P8, K1.

Row 6: Sl1, K11.

Continuing with MC yarn and a new needle, pick up 12 sts from the CO edge. Join these 12 sts into a round with your original 12 sts, for a total of 24 sts. Continue:

Round 1: Knit.

Round 2: [SSK, K3, M1R, K2, M1L, K3, K2tog] 2 times.

Round 3: [SSK, K8, K2tog] 2 times—20 sts.

Round 4: [SSK, K2, M1R, K2, M1L, K2, K2tog] 2 times.

Round 5: [SSK, K6, K2tog] 2 times—16 sts.

Round 6: [SSK, K1, M1R, K2, M1L, K1, K2tog] 2 times.

Round 7: [SSK, K4, K2tog] 2 times—12 sts.

Lightly stuff the head with fiberfill. Continue:

Round 8: [SSK, M1R, K2, M1L, K2tog] 2 times.

Round 9: [SSK, K2, K2tog] 2 times—8 sts.

Round 10: [SSK, K2tog] 2 times—4 sts.

Cut yarn, thread through remaining 4 sts, and pull tight.

Eyes

You will be working the eyes directly onto the head. To work the left eye, use CC to pick up sts on the left side of the head, as follows: 11 sts at a diagonal across the front of the face, 5 sts along the top edge, and another 5 sts along the side edge for a total of 21 sts. Use **Figure 9** for guidance in picking up these sts.

Figure 9

Join these sts into a round and continue:

Rounds 1 & 2: Knit.

Round 3: K2tog 3 times, K1, K2tog 4 times, K2, K2tog 2 times—12 sts.

Round 4: Knit.

Round 5: K2tog 6 times—6 sts.

Cut yarn, thread through remaining 6 sts, and pull tight.

To work the right eye, begin from the top of the head, and pick up sts symmetrically to the sts picked up for the left eye. Use **Figure 10** for guidance in picking up these sts.

Figure 10

Work rounds 1–5 as above for left eye.

Finishing

Sew head onto the top of the thorax, using model as a guide to placement. If desired, attach two short ends of yarn to the top of the head as antennae. Take care of any loose yarn ends.

Ants

These ubiquitous critters are just about everywhere, and I couldn't bring myself to create a collection of garden amigurumi without including them. And, of course, you don't need to stop with knitting up just one! Knit up a whole colony of these little guys for some real backyard fun!

yarn
Worsted weight
MC (dark red or sienna): 60 yd (55 m)
Shown: Cascade 220 color #9404 or 8884
CC (brilliant orange): less than 5 yd (4.5 m) (optional)

needles
· One set U.S. size 5 (3.75 mm) double-pointed needles
  and/or
· Two U.S. size 5(3.75 mm) circular needles,
  24" (61 cm) long

notions
· Fiberfill stuffing
· Tapestry needle
· Six chenille stems

gauge
22 to 24 sts = 4" (10 cm) in stockinette stitch

dimensions
Length: 6" (15 cm)

difficulty
Intermediate/Experienced

Pattern

Front and Middle Leg *(Make 4)*

In MC, CO 25 sts. Continue, working in rows:

Row 1: Sl1, P8, w&t.

Row 2: K8, P1.

Row 3: Sl1, P18, w&t.

Row 4: K7, w&t.

Row 5: P11, w&t.

Row 6: K2, w&t.

Row 7: P3, K1.

BO all sts. Cut yarn, leaving a long tail. Using tapestry needle, sew (whip st) the CO edge of the work to the BO edge of the work.

Hind Legs *(Make 2)*

In MC, CO 30 sts. Continue, working in rows:

Row 1: Sl1, P9, w&t.

Row 2: K9, P1.

Row 3: Sl1, P22, w&t.

Row 4: K10, w&t.

Row 5: P15, w&t.

Row 6: K3, w&t.

Row 7: P4, K1.

BO all sts. Cut yarn, leaving a long tail. Using this long yarn tail and a tapestry needle, sew (whip st) the CO edge of the work to the BO edge.

Head & Antenna

In MC, CO 14 sts. Continue, working in rows:

Row 1: Sl1, P11, w&t.

Row 2: K10, w&t.

Row 3: P9, w&t.

Row 4: K8, w&t.

Row 5: P10, K1.

Row 6: Sl1, K13.

Turn the work. Using a new needle and continuing with MC yarn, pick up 14 additional sts along the CO edge of the work. You should now have a total of 28 sts.

Join these 28 sts into a round, and continue:

Round 1: Knit.

Round 2: [SSK, K4, M1R, K2, M1L, K4, K2tog] 2 times.

Round 3: [SSK, K10, K2tog] 2 times—24 sts.

Round 4: [SSK, K3, M1R, K2, M1L, K3, K2tog] 2 times—24 sts.

Round 5: [SSK, K8, K2tog] 2 times—20 sts.

Round 6: [SSK, K2, M1R, K2, M1L, K2, K2tog] 2 times—20 sts.

Round 7: [SSK, K6, K2tog] 2 times—16 sts.

Round 8: [SSK, K1, M1R, K2, M1L, K1, K2tog] 2 times—16 sts.

Round 9: [SSK, K4, K2tog] 2 times—12 sts.

Round 10: [SSK, M1R, K2, M1L, K2tog] 2 times—12 sts.

Stuff head with fiberfill. Do not overstuff.

Round 11: [SSK, K2, K2tog] 2 times—8 sts.

Round 12: [SSK, K2tog] 2 times—4 sts.

Cut yarn, thread through remaining 4 sts, and pull tight.

To work right antenna, pick up 4 sts in a circle at the right side of the head, using model as a guide. Work 20 rows of I-chord. Cut yarn, thread through final 4 sts, and thread through the tip of the antenna to create a blunt tip. Work left antenna analogously to right antenna.

Top of Thorax

In MC, CO 8 sts. Continue, working in rows:

Row 1: Sl1, P5, w&t.

Row 2: K4, w&t.

Row 3: P3, w&t.

Row 4: K2, w&t.

Row 5: P4, K1.

Row 6: Sl1, K7.

Row 7: Sl1, P6, K1.

Rows 8 & 9: Repeat rows 6 & 7.

Row 10: Sl1, K1, K2tog, SSK, K2—6 sts.

Row 11: Sl1, P4, K1.

Row 12: Sl1, K5.

Row 13: Repeat row 11.

Row 14: Sl1, K2tog, SSK, K1—4 sts.

Rows 15 & 17: Sl1, P2, K1.

Row 16 & 18: Sl1, K3.

BO all sts.

Abdomen

CO 4 sts in MC. Join these sts into a round, and continue:

Round 1: K-fb 4 times—8 sts.

Round 2: Knit.

Round 3: [K1, KLL, KRL, K1] 4 times—16 sts.

Round 4: Knit.

Round 5: [K1, M1L, K2, M1R, K1] 4 times—24 sts.

Round 6: Knit.

Round 7: K5, M1R, K2, M1L, K17—26 sts.

Round 8: Knit.

Round 9: K6, M1R, K2, M1L, K18—28 sts.

Rounds 10–15: Knit.

Round 16: K6, K2tog, SSK, K18—26 sts.

Round 17: Knit.

Round 18: K5, K2tog, SSK, K17—24 sts.

Round 19: Knit.

Round 20: K4, K2tog, SSK, K4, SSK, K8, K2tog—20 sts.

Round 21: Knit.

Round 22: K3, K2tog, SSK, K3, SSK, K6, K2tog—16 sts.

Round 23: Knit.

Round 24: K2, K2tog, SSK, K2, SSK, K4, K2tog—12 sts.

Round 25: Knit.

Stuff the abdomen with fiberfill. Do not overstuff. Continue:

Round 26: K1, K2tog, SSK, K1, SSK, K2, K2tog—8 sts.

Round 27: Knit.

Round 28: K2tog, SSK, SSK, K2tog—4 sts.

Cut yarn, thread through remaining 4 sts and pull tight.

Thorax & Abdomen Assembly

First, use Figure 1 as a guide to attach the top of thorax to the abdomen.

Next, use Figure 2 as a guide to sew all 6 legs to the selvedges of the thorax. Note that you will be sewing the upper selvedge of each of the legs to the selvedges of the thorax.

Next, turn the assembly over and pick up 16 sts around the underside opening of the thorax as follows: 2 sts on the left side of the abdomen, 1 st on the selvedge of the thorax in between the abdomen and left hind leg, 1 st on the seam of the left hind leg, 3 sts on the selvedge of the

Figure 1

Figure 2

thorax in between the left hind leg and the left middle leg, 1 st on the seam of the left middle leg, 3 sts on the selvedge of the thorax in between the left middle leg and the left front leg, 1 st on the seam of the left front leg, and 4 sts on the CO edge of the thorax. Note that the sts picked up from the CO edge of the thorax only extend to the midpoint of this edge. Use Figure 3 as a guide when picking up these sts.

Continue, working in rows, as follows:

Row 1: Sl1, P11, w&t.

Row 2: K10, w&t.

Row 3: P7, w&t.

Row 4: K5, w&t.

Row 5: P11, K1.

Row 6: Sl1, K15.

Figure 3

Continuing with MC yarn and a second needle, pick up another 16 sts from the opposite selvedge of the thorax. Be sure to pick up these sts symmetrically to the sts picked up on the left side of the thorax: 4 sts on the CO edge of the thorax, 1 st on the seam of the right front leg, 3 sts on the selvedge of the thorax between the right front leg and the right middle leg, 1 st on the seam of the right middle leg, 3 sts on the selvedge of the thorax between the right middle leg and the right hind leg, 1 st on the seam of the right hind leg, 1 st on the selvedge of the thorax between the right hind leg and the abdomen, and 2 sts from the abdomen.

Cut yarn, leaving a long tail. Using a tapestry needle and this long yarn tail, graft the sts from the first needle to the sts on the second needle. While grafting, lightly stuff the thorax with fiberfill. If you desire pose-able legs, insert chenille stems, blunt end first, into each of the six legs.

Finishing

Sew the head onto the thorax. Optional: Use CC yarn to embroider eyes onto the head. Take care of any loose yarn ends.

Garden Snail

If I had my own garden, I'm sure that I would consider these little creatures to be pests of the worst variety. A crew of these hungry beasts can eat through any vegetable garden, destroying the labors of a whole season. On the other hand, there's something endearing about their slow slide through life, their shy little eyes peeking out from under their solid shells. I hope that this knitted mollusk conjures up the charming aspects rather than the pesky ones.

yarn

Worsted weight
Shell Color 1 (SC1) (deep aqua): 25 yd (23 m)
Shown: Cascade 220 color #9420
Shell Color 2 (SC2) (bright aqua): 50 yd (46 m)
Shown: Cascade 220 color #8891
Shell Color 3 (SC3) (bright turquoise): 50 yd (46 m)
Shown: Cascade 220 color #7812
Shell Color 4 (SIC4) (deep turquoise): 50 yd (46 m)
Shown: Cascade 220 color #7813
Mantle Main Color (MMC) (marigold): 75 yd (68.5 m)
Shown: Cascade 220 color #7826
Small amount of dark brown (for embroidering eye spots)

needles

• One set U.S. size 5 (3.75 mm) double-pointed needles
and/or
• Two U.S. size 5 (3.75 mm) circular needles,
24" (61 cm) long

notions

• One 12" (30.5 cm) chenille stem
• Fiberfill stuffing
• Tapestry needle
• Stitch holder

gauge

22 to 24 sts = 4" (10 cm) in stockinette stitch

dimensions

Mantle length: 8" (20 cm)
Shell diameter: 6" (15 cm)

difficulty

Intermediate/Experienced

Pattern

Shell

In SC1, CO 24 sts using the knit-on method.

Continue working back and forth in rows as follows:

Row 1: *K-tbl, repeat from * to end of row.

Row 2: Sl1 kwise, P2, w&t.

Row 3: K-fb, K1, P1.

Row 4: Sl1 kwise, P5, w&t.

Row 5: K-fb, K1, K-fb, K2, P1.

Row 6: Sl1 kwise, P9, w&t.

Row 7: K-fb, K1, K-fb, K2, K-fb, K3, P1.

Row 8: Sl1 kwise, P14, w&t.

Row 9: K-fb, K1, K-fb, K2, K-fb, K3, K-fb, K4, P1.

Cut SC1 yarn, and attach SC2 yarn.

Continue:

Row 10: Sl1 kwise, P20, w&t.

Row 11: K-fb, K1, K-fb, K2, K-fb, K3, K-fb, K4, K-fb, K5, P1.

Row 12: Sl1 kwise, P27, w&t.

Row 13: K-fb, K1, K-fb, K2, K-fb, K3, K-fb, K4, K-fb, K5, K-fb, K6, P1.

Row 14: Sl1 kwise, P35, w&t.

Row 15: K-fb, K1, K-fb, K2, K-fb, K3, K-fb, K4, K-fb, K5, K-fb, K6, K-fb, K7, P1.

Cut SC2 yarn, and attach SC3 yarn. Continue:

Row 16: Sl1 kwise, P44, w&t.

Row 17: K-fb, K1, K-fb, K2, K-fb, K3, K-fb, K4, K-fb, K5, K-fb, K6, K-fb, K7, K-fb, K8, P1.

Row 18: Sl1 kwise, P54, w&t.

Row 19: K-fb, K1, K-fb, K2, K-fb, K3, K-fb, K4, K-fb, K5, K-fb, K6, K-fb, K7, K-fb, K8, K-fb, K9, P1.

Cut SC3 yarn, and attach SC4 yarn.

Continue:

Row 20: Sl1 kwise, P65, w&t.

Row 21: K-fb, K1, K-fb, K2, K-fb, K3, K-fb, K4, K-fb, K5, K-fb, K6, K-fb, K7, K-fb, K8, K-fb, K9, K-fb, K10, P1.

Row 22: Sl1 kwise, P77, K1.

Row 23: Sl1 kwise, K-fb, K1, K-fb, K2, K-fb, K3, K-fb, K4, K-fb, K5, K-fb, K6, K-fb, K7, K-fb, K8, K-fb, K9, K-fb, K10, K-fb, K11, P1.

Cut SC4 yarn. Place these 90 sts on a stitch holder for later use.

Turn work. Using SC1 yarn, pick up 24 sts kwise from the right side of the CO edge.

Continue, working back and forth in rows, as follows:

Row 1: *P-tbl, repeat from * to end of row.

Row 2: Sl1 kwise, K1, K-fb, w&t.

Row 3: P4.

Row 4: Sl1 kwise, K1, K-fb, K2, K-fb, w&t.

Row 5: P8.

Row 6: Sl1 kwise, K1, K-fb, K3, K-fb, K2, K-fb, w&t.

Row 7: P13.

Row 8: Sl1 kwise, K1, K-fb, K4, K-fb, K3, K-fb, K2, K-fb, w&t.

Row 9: P19.

Cut SC1 yarn, and attach SC2 yarn.

Continue:

Row 10: Sl1 kwise, K1, K-fb, K5, K-fb, K4, K-fb, K3, K-fb, K2, K-fb, w&t.

Row 11: P26.

Row 12: Sl1 kwise, K1, K-fb, K6, K-fb, K5, K-fb, K4, K-fb, K3, K-fb, K2, K-fb, w&t.

Row 13: P34.

Row 14: Sl1 kwise, K1, K-fb, K7, K-fb, K6, K-fb, K5, K-fb, K4, K-fb, K3, K-fb, K2, K-fb, w&t.

Row 15: P43.

Cut SC2 yarn, and attach SC3 yarn.

Continue:

Row 16: Sl1 kwise, K1, K-fb, K8, K-fb, K7, K-fb, K6, K-fb, K5, K-fb, K4, K-fb, K3, K-fb, K2, K-fb, w&t.

Row 17: P53.

Row 18: Sl1 kwise, K1, K-fb, K9, K-fb, K8, K-fb, K7, K-fb, K6, K-fb, K5, K-fb, K4, K-fb, K3, K-fb, K2, K-fb, w&t.

Row 19: P64.

Cut SC3 yarn, and attach SC4 yarn.

Continue:

Row 20: Sl1 kwise, K1, K-fb, K10, K-fb, K9, K-fb, K8, K-fb, K7, K-fb, K6, K-fb, K5, K-fb, K4, K-fb, K3, K-fb, K2, K-fb, w&t.

Row 21: P76.

Row 22: Sl1 kwise, K1, K-fb, K11, K-fb, K10, K-fb, K9, K-fb, K8, K-fb, K7, K-fb, K6, K-fb, K5, K-fb, K4, K-fb, K3, K-fb, K2, K-fb, K1.

There should now be 90 sts on your needle. Cut SC4 yarn, leaving a long tail. Weave in any loose yarn ends.

If necessary, transfer 90 held sts from stitch holder onto a second needle. Using a tapestry needle and long yarn tail, graft (using Kitchener st) the 90 sts from the first needle to the 90 sts on the second needle. While grafting, lightly stuff the shell with fiberfill.

If desired, fold a chenille stem in half and use it to shape the inner corkscrew of the shell as you are stuffing. This will help maintain the integrity of the spiral, but is not mandatory.

Mantle

CO 12 sts in MMC. Continue in rows as follows:

Row 1: Sl1, P11.

Row 2: Sl1, K4, M1R, K2, M1L, K4, P1—14 sts.

Row 3: Sl1, P13.

Row 4: Sl1, K5, M1R, K2, M1L, K5, P1—16 sts.

Row 5: Sl1, P15.

Row 6: Sl1, K14, P1.

Row 7: Sl1, P15.

Row 8: Sl1, SSK, K10, K2tog, P1—14 sts.

Row 9: Sl1, P13.

Row 10: Sl1, SSK, K8, K2tog, P1—12 sts.

Row 11: Sl1, P2tog, P6, P2tog-tbls, P1—10 sts.

Row 12: Sl1, SSK, K4, K2tog, P1—8 sts.

Row 13: Sl1, P2tog, P2, P2tog-tbls, P1—6 sts.

Row 14: Sl1, K5.

Continue with MMC yarn, and pick up 9 sts kwise from the left selvedge of the work for a total of 15 sts. Turn work and continue:

Row 15: K11, P2, K2.

Continue with MMC yarn, and pick up 9 sts pwise from the right selvedge of the work, for a total of 24 sts. Turn work and continue:

Row 16: P24.

Row 17: Sl1, K22, P1.

Row 18: Sl1, P23.

Rows 19-64: Repeat rows 17 & 18, 23 times.

Row 65: Sl1, K9, K2tog, SSK, K9, P1—22 sts.

Row 66: Sl1, P21.

Row 67: Sl1, K8, K2tog, SSK, K8, P1—20 sts.

Row 68: Sl1, P19.

Row 69: Sl1, K7, K2tog, SSK, K7, P1—18 sts.

Row 70: Sl1, P17.

Row 71: Sl1, K6, K2tog, SSK, K6, P1—16 sts.

Row 72: Sl1, P15.

Row 73: Sl1, K5, K2tog, SSK, K5, P1—14 sts.

Row 74: Sl1, P13.

Row 75: Sl1, K4, K2tog, SSK, K4, P1—12 sts.

Row 76: Sl1, P11.

Row 77: Sl1, K3, K2tog, SSK, K3, P1—10 sts.

Row 78: Sl1, P9.

Row 79: Sl1, K2, K2tog, SSK, K2, P1—8 sts.

Row 80: Sl1, P7.

Row 81: Sl1, K1, K2tog, SSK, K1, P1—6 sts.

Row 82: Sl1, P5.

Row 83: Sl1, K2tog, SSK, P1—4 sts.

Row 84: Sl1, P3.

Row 85: K2tog, SSK—2 sts.

Cut yarn, thread through remaining 2 sts and pull tight.

Turn work over. Using **Figure 1** as a guide, pick up a total of 103 sts in MMC from the circumference of the mantle. Pick up sts as follows: 46 sts from the right selvedge of the work, 11 sts from the CO edge, and another 46 sts from the left selvedge of the work. When picking up sts from the selvedges, pick up the sts approximately 2 or 3 st columns inside of the selvedge. This will allow the edge of the mantle to flare outward, creating a neat roll of sts. When picking up sts from the CO edge, pick them up at the edge of the wrong side of the work, leaving the CO edge visible.

Figure 1

Cut yarn. Slip first 24 sts from the right selvedge of the work onto a new needle. Reattach MMC and continue working back and forth along the periphery of the mantle:

Row 1: K61, w&t.

Row 2: P73, w&t.

Row 3: K85, w&t.

Row 4: P37, P2tog 4 times, P1, P2tog 4 times, P40, w&t—95 sts.

Row 5: K40, K2tog 2 times, K1, K2tog 2 times, K43—91 sts.

Cut yarn, leaving a long tail. Divide sts onto two needles, placing 42 sts on first needle and 43 stss on a second needle. With long yarn tail and a tapestry needle, graft (using Kitchener st) the sts from the first needle to the sts on the second needle. While grafting, stuff the mantle lightly with fiberfill.

Eyestalks

To work left eye stalk, use MMC, and pick up 8 sts in a ring on the left side of the head region of the mantle. Use **Figure 2** as a guide.

Figure 2

Join these sts in a round and continue:

Round 1: Knit.

Round 2: K2tog 4 times—4 sts.

Rounds 3–9: Knit.

Round 10: [KRL, K2, KLL] 2 times—8 sts.

Rounds 11 & 12: Knit.

Round 13: K2tog 4 times—4 sts.

Cut yarn, thread through remaining 4 sts and pull tight.

To work right eyestalk, use MMC and pick up 8 sts in a ring on the right side of the head region. Make sure that the positioning of these sts is symmetrical to the position of the sts picked up when working the left eyestalk. Join these sts in a round and work Rounds 1–13 as for left eyestalk.

Use dark brown yarn and tapestry needle to embroider eyes on the end of the eyestalks. Use the photo on page 93 as guide for placement.

Whiskers

Work the left whisker by picking up 4 sts in a ring formation on the left side of the head. Use **Figure 3** as a guide.

Figure 3

Join into a round and work as follows:

Rounds 1–4: Knit.

Cut yarn, thread through remaining sts and pull tight. Use tapestry needle and thread tail of yarn through the tip of the whisper to create a slightly bulbous point.

Work the right whisker identically to the left whisker by picking up 4 sts on the right side of the head.

Finishing

Sew shell onto mantle. Lift up the lip of the shell, and using tapestry needle and MMC yarn, sew the mantle to the inner surface of the shell. Take care of any loose yarn ends.

Spider

Unlike the delicate Miss Muffett, I've never found spiders particularly frightening. Even so, spiders are highly specialized predators, lying in wait within their wispy webs with venom-laced fangs agape. This knit version is sans poison but filled with attitude. The legs can be made pose-able with chenille stems or left soft for the safety of a young child. Either way, this sweet critter makes a charming companion!

yarn

Worsted weight
C1 (raspberry violet): 75 yd (68.5 m)
Shown: Cascade 220 color #9474
C2 (royal purple): 25 yd (23 m)
Shown: Cascade 220 color #8114
C3 (dusty rose): 25 yd (23 m)
Shown: Cascade 220 color #8834

needles

- Two sets U.S. size 5 (3.75 mm) double-pointed needles
and/or
- Two U.S. size 5 (3.75 mm) circular needles, 24" (61 cm) long

notions

- Eight 12" (30.5 cm) chenille stems (optional)
- Fiberfill stuffing
- Tapestry needle

gauge

22 to 24 sts = 4" (10 cm) in stockinette stitch

dimensions

Body length: 8" (20 cm)

difficulty

Intermediate/
Experienced

Pattern

Legs (Make 8)

In C1, CO 36 sts. Continue, working back and forth in rows, as follows:

Row 1 (wrong side): Sl1, P12, w&t.

Row 2 (right side): K12, P1.

Row 3: Sl1, P3, w&t.

Row 4: K3, P1.

Row 5: Sl1, P11, w&t.

Row 6: K11, P1.

Row 7: Sl1, P2, w&t.

Row 8: K2, P1.

Row 9: Sl1, P26, w&t.

Row 10: K11, w&t.

Row 11: P10, w&t.

Row 12: K11, w&t.

Row 13: P19, w&t.

Row 14: K4, w&t.

Row 15: P2, w&t.

Row 16: K3, w&t.

Row 17: P6, K1.

BO all sts. Cut yarn, leaving a long tail. Using a tapestry needle and this long yarn tail, whip st the CO edge to the BO edge. When doing this, sew just inside the CO and BO edges so that the st definition on the edges is still visible following sewing.

Abdomen

In C1, CO 18 sts. Join these sts into a round and continue:

Round 1: Knit.

Round 2: K1, M1L, K4, M1R, K1, [K1, M1L, K2, M1R, K1] 3 times—26 sts.

Round 3: Knit.

Attach C2 yarn. Work rounds 4, 8, 12, 16, 20, 24, 28, 32, and 36 in C2. All other rounds should be worked in C1.

Round 4 (in C2): K1, M1L, K6, M1R, K1, [K1, M1L, K4, M1R, K1] 3 times—34 sts.

Round 5: Knit.

Round 6: K1, M1L, K8, M1R, K1, [K1, M1L, K6, M1R, K1] 3 times—42 sts.

Round 7: Knit.

Round 8 (in C2): K1, M1L, K10, M1R, K1, [K1, M1L, K8, M1R, K1] 3 times—50 sts.

Round 9: Knit.

Round 10: K1, M1L, K12, M1R, K1, [K1, M1L, K10, M1R, K1] 3 times—58 sts.

Round 11: Knit.

Round 12 (in C2): K1, M1L, K14, M1R, K1, [K1, M1L, K12, M1R, K1] 3 times—66 sts.

Rounds 13–20 (16 and 20 in C2): Knit.

Round 21: SSK, K14, K2tog, [SSK, K20, K2tog] 2 times—60 sts.

Round 22: Knit.

Round 23: K16, [SSK, K18, K2tog] 2 times—56 sts.

Round 24 (in C2): SSK, K12, K2tog, K40—54 sts.

Round 25: K14, [SSK, K16, K2tog] 2 times—50 sts.

Round 26: Knit.

Round 27: SSK, K10, K2tog, [SSK, K14, K2tog] 2 times—44 sts.

Round 28 (in C2): Knit.

Round 29: K12, [SSK, K12, K2tog] 2 times—40 sts.

Round 30: SSK, K8, K2tog, K28—38 sts.

Round 31: K10, [SSK, K10, K2tog] 2 times—34 sts.

Round 32 (in C2): Knit.

Round 33: SSK, K6, K2tog, [SSK, K8, K2tog] 2 times—28 sts.

Round 34: Knit.

Round 35: K8, [SSK, K6, K2tog] 2 times—24 sts.

Round 36 (in C2): SSK, K4, K2tog, K16—22 sts.

Round 37: K6, [SSK, K4, K2tog] 2 times—18 sts.

Round 38: Knit.

Round 39: [SSK, K2, K2tog] 3 times—12 sts.

Round 40: Knit.

Round 41: K4, [SSK, K2tog] 2 times—8 sts.

Round 42: SSK, K2tog, K4—6 sts.

Round 43: K2, K2tog, SSK—4 sts.

Cut yarn, thread through final 6 sts and pull tight.

Chelicerae *(Make 2)*

Work the chelicerae (fangs), as follows. In C3, CO 14 sts. Work in rows as follows:

Row 1: Sl1, P5, w&t.

Row 2: K4, w&t.

Row 3: P6, w&t.

Row 4: K8.

Now, join the sts in a round and continue:

Round 5: Knit.

Round 6: K6, SSK, K4, K2tog—12 sts.

Round 7: Knit.

Round 8: [SSK, K2, K2tog] 2 times—8 sts.

Round 9: Knit.

Round 10: [SSK, K2tog] 2 times—4 sts.

Round 11: Knit.

Cut yarn, thread through final 4 sts and pull tight.

Assembly of Cephalothorax

Using C1, pick up sts consecutively as follows: 2 sts from the upper selvedge of two legs (to total 4 sts), 7 sts from the upper selvedge of each chelicerae (to total 14 sts) and 2 sts from the upper selvedge of two legs (to total 4 sts). This will result in a total of 22 sts. See **Figure 1** for guidance in picking up these sts.

Figure 1

Continue, working back and forth in rows, as follows:

Row 1: Sl1, P15, w&t.

Row 2: K6, w&t.

Row 3: P8, w&t.

Row 4: K10, w&t.

Row 5: P12, w&t.

Row 6: K14, w&t.

Row 7: P15, w&t.

Row 8: K16, w&t.

Row 9: P17, w&t.

Row 10: K18, w&t.

Row 11: P12, w&t.

Rows 12–20: Repeat rows 2–10.

Row 21: P19, K1.

Row 22: Sl1, K21.

Continuing with C1 yarn and a new needle, pick up sts consecutively as follows: 2 sts from the upper selvedge of two legs (to total 4 sts), 14 sts from around the upper CO region of the abdomen, and 2 sts from the upper selvedge of two legs (to total 4 sts). This will result in a total of 22 sts. See **Figure 2** for guidance in picking up this second set of 22 sts.

Figure 2

Join these sts into a round with the original 22 sts, for a total of 44 sts. Knit one round. Cut yarn, leaving a long tail. Using the long yarn tail and a tapestry needle, graft (Kitchener st) the sts from the first needle to the sts on the second needle.

Underside of Cephalothorax

Turn over the work. Using C3 yarn, pick up 56 sts from around the open perimeter of the cephalothorax as follows: 8 sts from the underside of one chelicerae, 4 sts from the underside of each of four legs (to total 16 sts), 8 sts from the underside opening of the abdomen, 4 sts from the underside of each of four legs (to total 16 sts) and 8 sts from the underside of the second chelicerae. Use **Figure 3** for clarification in picking up these 56 sts.

Figure 3

Join these sts in a round, and proceed:

Rounds 1–4: Knit.

Stuff the cephalothorax with fiberfill. If desired, insert chenille stems into each of the eight legs. Create a blunt end by folding a 1" (2.5 cm) section of the stem over and twisting it tightly with its overlapping section. Insert the stem, blunt end first, into the leg. Once you have inserted stems into each of the legs, twist the sharp ends of the stems around each other to create a tight, compact ball. Wrap with generous quantities of waste yarn and distribute fiberfill to create adequate padding. Continue:

Round 5: *K2tog, repeat from * to end of round—28 sts.

Round 6: Knit.

Round 7: *K2tog, repeat from * to end of round—14 sts.

Round 8: *K2tog 3 times, K1, repeat from * to end of round—8 sts.

Cut yarn, thread through final 8 sts and pull tight.

Finishing

Use C2 yarn, and embroider eight eyes onto cephalothorax. Use model for guidance. Take care of any loose yarn ends.

Revenge of the Cryptids:
strange, mythical, cryptozoological specimens

The dictionary defines cryptozoology as "the search for or study of animals whose existence or survival is disputed or unsubstantiated." Now, you can be uber-geeky and knit up your very own menagerie of amigurumi cryptids. Keep them or gift them. After all, nothing says 'I love you' better than a hand-knit jackalope!

Kraken

Krakens were popular in the tall tales of marine adventurers. They remained there until the 1800s, merely fiction and speculation, until a humungous mollusk-ean carcass washed up on a beach in England under the nose of the British Naturalist Society. After that fateful event, the Kraken was no longer a myth, but a creature known to science as the giant squid, Architeuthis Dux. I still prefer the name Kraken. It has a much more ferocious ring to it, and seems to fit the diabolical intentions of this knitted creature much more than the timid and slow-moving Architeuthis!

yarn

Worsted weight
MC (burnt orange multi): yd (100.5 m)
Shown: Cascade 220 Paints color #9928
CC (dusty coral): 40 yd (36.5 m)
Shown: Cascade 220 color #4146
Eye Color 1 (EC1) (ebony brown): less than 20 yd (18 m)
Eye Color 2 (EC2) (natural white): less than 20 yd (18 m)

needles

· One set U.S. size 5 (3.75 mm) double-pointed needles
and/or
· Two U.S. size 5 (3.75 mm) circular needles
24" (61 cm) long

notions

· Fiberfill stuffing
· Tapestry needle
· Ten 12" (30.5 cm) chenille stems (optional)

gauge

22 to 24 sts = 4" (10 cm) in stockinette stitch

dimensions

Maximum tentacle length: 16" (40.5 cm)
Height: 11" (28 cm)

difficulty

Intermediate/Experienced

Pattern

Arms *(Make 8)*

CO 32 sts in CC. Change to MC and continue:

Row 1 (right side): Sl1, K30, P1.

Row 2: Sl1, P15, w&t.

Row 3: K15, P1.

Row 4: Sl1, P23, w&t.

Row 5: K23, P1.

Row 6: Sl1, P7, w&t.

Row 7: K7, P1.

Row 8: Sl1, P30, K1.

Cut MC yarn. Continue in CC:

Row 9: Sl1, K30, P1.

BO all sts. Cut CC yarn, leaving a long tail. Using a tapestry needle and this long yarn tail, whip st the CO edge to the BO edge.

Grasping Tentacles *(Make 2)*

CO 48 in CC. Continue:

Row 1: Sl1, P11, w&t.

Row 2: K10, w&t.

Row 3: P9, w&t.

Row 4: K7, w&t.

Row 5: P6, w&t.

Row 6: K4, w&t.

Row 7: P3, w&t.

Row 8: K9.

Attach MC yarn. Continue in MC:

Row 9: Sl1, K46, P1.

Row 10: Sl1, P31, w&t.

Row 11: K31, P1.

Row 12: Sl1, P41, w&t.

Row 13: K3, w&t.

Row 14: P5, w&t.

Row 15: K6, w&t.

Row 16: P8, w&t.

Row 17: K9, w&t.

Row 18: P10, K1.

Row 19: Sl1, K11, w&t.

Row 20: P10, w&t.

Row 21: K9, w&t.

Row 22: P7, w&t.

Row 23: K6, w&t.

Row 24: P4, w&t.

Row 25: K3, w&t.

Row 26: P8, K1.

Cut MC yarn. Continue in CC:

Row 27: Sl1, K11, w&t.

Row 28: K6, w&t.

Row 29: P3, w&t.

Row 30: K5, w&t.

Row 31: P6, w&t.

Row 32: K8, w&t.

Row 33: P9, w&t.

Row 34: K11.

Row 35: Sl1, P11, K35, P1.

BO all sts. Cut CC yarn, leaving a long tail. Using tapestry needle and this long yarn tail, sew (whip stitch) the CO edge to the BO edge.

Assembly of Arms and Tentacles

Using MC yarn, pick up sts on the selvedges of the arms and grasping tentacles as follows: 3 sts from the selvedges of four arms (to total 12 sts), 2 sts from the selvedge of one grasping tentacle, 3 sts from the selvedges of four arms (to total 12 sts), and 2 sts from the selvedge of one grasping tentacle. Use **Figure 1** for guidance. You should now have a total of 28 sts.

Figure 1

Join these sts into a round, and continue:

Rounds 1–16: Knit.

To close the underside of the assembly, use a tapestry needle and a length of yarn in CC to st together the inside edges of the arms and tentacles. See **Figure 2** for guidance.

Figure 2

If desired, insert folded chenille stems, blunt end first, into each of the arms and tentacles. Twist the protruding ends around each other, and wrap with waste yarn. Stuff the assembly with fiberfill. Continue, still working in MC, as follows:

Round 17: *K5, K2tog, repeat from * to end of round—24 sts.

Round 18: *K4, K2tog, repeat from * to end of round—20 sts.

Round 19: *K3, K2tog, repeat from * to end of round—16 sts.

Round 20: *K2, K2tog, repeat from * to end of round—12 sts.

Round 21: *K1, K2tog, repeat from * to end of round—8 sts.

Round 22: *K2tog, repeat from * to end of round—4 sts.

Cut yarn, thread through remaining 4 sts, and pull tight.

Mantle

In MC, pick up 28 sts around the upper crown of the arm and tentacle assembly. Begin picking up these sts directly above one of the grasping tentacles. Use **Figure 3** for guidance.

Figure 3

Join these sts into a round and continue:

Round 1: Purl.

Round 2: *K-fb, K1, repeat from * to end of round—42 sts.

Rounds 3–35: Knit.

Round 36: *SSK, K17, K2tog, repeat from * to end of round—38 sts.

Round 37: Knit.

Round 38: *SSK, K15, K2tog, repeat from * to end of round—34 sts.

Round 39: Knit.

Round 40: *SSK, K13, K2tog, repeat from * to end of round—30 sts.

Round 41: Knit.

Round 42: *SSK, K11, K2tog, repeat from * to end of round—26 sts.

Round 43: Knit.

Round 44: *SSK, K9, K2tog, repeat from * to end of round—22 sts.

Round 45: Knit.

Stuff mantle with generous quantities of fiberfill. Continue working mantle as follows:

Round 46: *SSK, K7, K2tog, repeat from * to end of round—18 sts.

Round 47: Knit.

Round 48: *SSK, K5, K2tog, repeat from * to end of round—14 sts.

Round 49: Knit.

Round 50: *SSK, K3, K2tog, repeat from * to end of round—10 sts.

Round 51: Knit.

Round 52: *SSK, K1, K2tog, repeat from * to end of round—6 sts.

Round 53: Knit.

Round 54: Sl2-K1-P2SSO 2 times—2 sts.

Cut yarn, thread through final 2 sts and pull tight.

Fins

Starting from the tip of the mantle, and continuing along one of the lateral decrease lines, pick up a total of 22 sts in MC. You will be picking up sts at the rate of one st per row along the decrease line. Turn the work. Continuing with MC, pick up another 22 sts directly behind the original 22 sts, for a total of 44 sts.

Join these sts into a round, and continue:

Round 1: Knit.

Round 2: *SSK, K18, K2tog, repeat from * to end of round—40 sts.

Round 3: *SSK, K16, K2tog, repeat from * to end of round—36 sts.

Round 4: *SSK, K14, K2tog, repeat from * to end of round—32 sts.

Round 5: *SSK, K12, K2tog, repeat from * to end of round—28 sts.

Round 6: *SSK, K10, K2tog, repeat from * to end of round—24 sts.

Round 7: *SSK, K8, K2tog, repeat from * to end of round—20 sts.

Round 8: *SSK, K6, K2tog, repeat from * to end of round—16 sts.

Round 9: *SSK, K4, K2tog, repeat from * to end of round—12 sts.

Round 10: *SSK, K2, K2tog, repeat from * to end of round—8 sts.

Round 11: *SSK, K2tog, repeat from * to end of round—4 sts.

Cut yarn, thread though final 4 sts, and pull tight.

Work a second fin on the opposite side of the mantle similarly to the first. This time, you will be picking up sts along the second decrease line on the side of the mantle.

Eyes *(Make 2)*

In EC1, CO 4 sts. Join these sts into a round, and continue:

Round 1: *K-fb, repeat from * to end of round—8 sts.

Round 2: Knit.

Round 3: *K-fb, repeat from * to end of round—16 sts.

Round 4: Knit.

Cut EC1 yarn, and attach EC2 yarn. Continue:

Round 5: *K-fb, repeat from * to end of round—32 sts.

Round 6: Knit.

BO all sts. Cut EC2 yarn, leaving a long yarn tail. Weave in any loose yarn ends.

Finishing

Using the long yarn tail on each of the eyes, sew each eye onto opposite sides of the head. Use a combination of mattress st and grafting. Take care of any loose yarn ends.

Nessie

Though I've never actually seen Nessie before, eyewitnesses report a bizarre creature with both flippers and legs, horns and fishlike tails, hooves and stripes. There are even some reports of paranormal disturbances when Nessie shows up, which really complicates the picture of what this elusive cryptid really looks like. This version is just my own fanciful rendition of the many possibilities. Much of it is worked in one piece, with extensive short row shaping. The appendages either can be worked directly on the finished creature, as in the pattern, or can be cast-on separately and sewn to your finished critter.

yarn
Worsted weight
MC (deep olive): 125 yd (114.5 m)
Shown: Cascade 220 color #9429
CC (lime gray): 50 yd (45.5 m)
Shown: Cascade 220 color #8229
Small amount of dark brown for eyes

needles
· One set U.S. size 5 (3.75 mm) double-pointed needles
  and/or
· Two U.S. size 5 (3.75 mm) circular needles,
  24" (61 cm) long

notions
· Fiberfill stuffing
· Row counter (optional, but recommended)
· Tapestry needle

gauge
22 to 24 sts = 4" (10 cm) in stockinette stitch

dimensions
Length: 14" (35.5 cm)
Maximum girth: 5" (12.5 cm)

difficulty
Intermediate

Pattern

Body

In MC, CO 4 sts. Continue, working in rows, as follows:

Rows 1, 3, 5, 7, 9: Sl1 kwise, P2, K1.

Rows 2, 4, 6, 8: Sl1 kwise, K3.

Row 10: Sl1 kwise, K1, KLL, KLR, K2—6 sts.

Rows 11, 13, 15, 17: Sl1 kwise, P4, K1.

Rows 12, 14, 16: Sl1 kwise, K5.

Row 18: Sl1 kwise, K1, M1L, K2, M1R, K2—8 sts.

Rows 19, 21, 23, 25: Sl1 kwise, P6, K1.

Rows 20, 22, 24: Sl1 kwise, K7.

Row 26: Sl1 kwise, K1, M1L, K4, M1R, K2—10 sts.

Rows 27, 29, 31, 33: Sl1 kwise, P8, K1.

Rows 28, 30, 32: Sl1 kwise, K9.

Row 34: Sl1 ktwise, K1, M1L, K6, M1R, K2—12 sts.

Rows 35, 37, 39, 41: Sl1 kwise, P10, K1.

Rows 36, 38, 40: Sl1 kwise, K11.

Row 42: Sl1 kwise, K1, M1L, K8, M1R, K2—14 sts.

Rows 43, 45, 47, 49: Sl1 kwise, P12, K1.

Rows 44, 46, 48: Sl1 kwise, K13.

Row 50: Sl1 kwise, K1, M1L, K10, M1R, K2—16 sts.

Rows 51, 53, 55, 57: Sl1 kwise, P14, K1.

Rows 52, 54, 56: Sl1 kwise, K15.

Rows 58: Sl1 kwise, K1, M1L, K12, M1R, K2—18 sts.

Row 59: Sl1 kwise, P16, K1.

Row 60: Sl1 kwise, K17.

Row 61: Sl1 kwise, P4, w&t.

Row 62: K5.

Row 63: Sl1 kwise, P6, w&t.

Row 64: K7.

Row 65: Sl1 kwise, P5, w&t.

Row 66: K6.

Row 67: Sl1 kwise, P16, K1.

Row 68: Sl1 kwise, K4, w&t.

Row 69: P4, K1.

Row 70: Sl1 kwise, K6, w&t.

Row 71: P6, K1.

Row 72: Sl1 kwise, K5, w&t.-

Row 73: P5, K1.

Row 74: Sl1, K1, M1L, K14, M1R, K2—20 sts.

Row 75: Sl1, P18, K1.

Row 76: Sl1, K1, M1L, K7, M1R, K2, M1L, K7, M1R, K2—24 sts.

Row 77: Sl1, P22, K1.

Row 78: Sl1, K1, M1L, K9, M1R, K2, M1L, K9, M1R, K2—28 sts.

Row 79: Sl1, P26, K1.

Row 80: Sl1, K12, M1R, K2, M1L, K13—30 sts.

Row 81: Sl1, P28, K1.

Row 82: Sl1, K20, w&t.

Row 83: P12, w&t.

Row 84: K17, w&t.

Row 85: P22, w&t.

Row 86: K26.

Rows 87, 89, & 91: Sl1, P28, K1.

Rows 88 & 90: Sl1, K29.

Row 92: Sl1, SSK, K24, K2tog, K1—28 sts.

Rows 93 & 95: Sl1, P26, K1.

Row 94: Sl1, K27.

Row 96: Sl1, SSK, K22, K2tog, K1—26 sts.

Rows 97 & 99: Sl1, P24, K1.

Row 98: Sl1, K25.

Row 100: Sl1, SSK, K20, K2tog, K1—24 sts.

Rows 101 & 103: Sl1, P22, K1.

Row 102: Sl1, K23.

Row 104: Sl1, SSK, K18, K2tog, K1—22 sts.

Rows 105 & 107: Sl1, P20, K1.

Row 106: Sl1, K21.

Row 108: Sl1, SSK, K16, K2tog, K1—20 sts.

Row 109: Sl1, P5, w&t.

Row 110: K6.

Row 111: Sl1, P18, K1.

Row 112: Sl1, K5, w&t.

Row 113: P5, K1.

Row 114: Sl1, SSK, K14, K2tog, K1—18 sts.

Row 115: Sl1, P5, w&t.

Row 116: K6.

Row 117: Sl1, P16, K1.

Row 118: Sl1, K5, w&t.

Row 119: P5, K1.

Row 120: Sl1, SSK, K12, K2tog, K1—16 sts.

Row 121: Sl1, P5, w&t.

Row 122: K6.

Row 123: Sl1, P14, K1.

Row 124: Sl1, K5, w&t.

Row 125: P5, K1.

Row 126: Sl1, SSK, K10, K2tog, K1—14 sts.

Row 127: Sl1, P4, w&t.

Row 128: K5.

Row 129: Sl1, P12, K1.

Row 130: Sl1, K4, w&t.

Row 131: P4, K1.

Row 132: Sl1, SSK, K8, K2tog, K1—12 sts.

Row 133: Sl1, P3, w&t.

Row 134: K4.

Row 135: Sl1, P10, K1.

Row 136: Sl1, K3, w&t.

Row 137: P3, K1.

Row 138: Sl1, SSK, K6, K2tog, K1—10 sts.

Row 139: Sl1, P2, w&t.

Row 140: K3.

Row 141: Sl1, P8, K1.

Row 142: Sl1, K2, w&t.

Row 143: P2, K1.

Row 144: Sl1, SSK, K4, K2tog, K1—8 sts.

Rows 145, 147, 149, 151, 153, 155, 157, 159, & 161: Sl1, P6, K1.

Rows 146, 148, 150, 152, 154, 156, 158, & 160: Sl1, K7.

Row 162: Sl1, K1, M1L, K4, M1R, K2—10 sts.

Row 163: Sl1, P6, w&t.

Row 164: K1, M1R, K2, M1L, K1, w&t—12 sts.

Row 165: P9, K1.

Row 166: Sl1, K11.

Row 167: Sl1, P8, w&t.

Row 168: K2, M1R, K2, M1L, K2, w&t—14 sts.

Row 169: P11, K1.

Row 170: Sl1, K13.

Join these 14 sts into a round, and continue with MC yarn:

Round 171: K5, K2tog, SSK, K5—12 sts.

Round 172: K12.

Round 173: K4, K2tog, SSK, K4—10 sts.

Round 174: K10.

Round 175: SSK, K1, K2tog, SSK, K1, K2tog—6 sts.

Cut yarn, thread through remaining 6 sts and pull tight.

Belly

Beginning at the selvedge under the chin, pick up a total of 66 sts in CC. Pick up 3 sts per 4 rows for these sts. Note that you will not be picking up sts at the selvedge at the tail region, but will be stopping around the region of the pelvis. See **Figure 1** for guidance in picking up these sts.

Continue working as follows:

Row 1: P21, w&t.

Row 2: K9, w&t.

Row 3: P15, w&t.

Row 4: K18, w&t.

Row 5: P24, w&t.

Row 6: K27, w&t.

Row 7: P33, w&t.

Row 8: K36, w&t.

Row 9: P19, w&t.

Row 10: K10, w&t.

Row 11: P17, w&t.

Row 12: K19, w&t.

Row 13: P26, w&t.

Figure 1

Row 14: K28, w&t.

Row 15: P35, w&t.

Row 16: K37, w&t.

Row 17: P19, w&t.

Rows 18–24: Repeat rows 2–8.

Row 25: P45, w&t.

Row 26: K48.

Continuing with CC yarn, use a new needle to pick up a total of 66 sts along the second selvedge of the work. Here, you will be beginning at the pelvis region, directly opposite the final picked up stitch on the first selvedge and moving to the region under the chin. Once again, you will be picking up 3 sts per 4 rows for these sts. You should now have a total of 132 sts on two needles. Cut yarn, leaving a lengthy tail. Using tapestry needle and this long tail, graft (Kitchener stitch) the sts on the first needle to the sts on the second needle. While you are doing this, stuff the body of your monster with fiberfill. Do not overstuff.

Front Flippers

Using **Figure 2** as a guide, pick up 6 sts in MC along the intersection between the body and belly at the shoulder region of you creature. Turn the work and pick up another 6 sts directly under the first 6 sts for a total of 12 sts.

Figure 2

Join these sts in a round and continue:

Round 1: Knit.

Round 2: *K1, M1L, K4, M1R, K1, repeat from * to end of round—16 sts.

Round 3: Knit.

Round 4: *K1, M1L, K6, M1R, K1, repeat from * to end of round—20 sts.

Round 5: Knit.

Rounds 6 & 8: SSK, K7, M1R, K2, M1L, K7, K2tog.

Rounds 7 & 9: Knit.

Round 10: *SSK, K6, K2tog, repeat from * to end of round—16 sts.

Round 11: Knit.

Round 12: *SSK, K4, K2tog, repeat from * to end of round—12 sts.

Round 13: Knit.

Round 14: *SSK, K2, K2tog, repeat from * to end of round—8 sts.

Round 15: Knit.

Round 16: *SSK, K2tog, repeat from * to end of round—4 sts.

Cut yarn, thread through remaining 4 sts, and pull tight.

Work opposite front flipper analogously by picking up 12 sts on the opposite side of the body and working rounds as above.

Back Flippers

Using **Figure 3** as a guide, pick up 12 sts in MC along the intersection between the body and belly at the pelvic region. Turn the work and pick up another 12 sts directly under the first 12 sts for a total of 24 sts.

Figure 3

Join these sts into a round and continue:

Round 1: Knit.

Round 2: *K1, M1L, K10, M1R, K1, repeat from * to end of round—28 sts.

Round 3: Knit.

Round 4: *K1, M1L, K12, M1R, K1, repeat from * to end of round—32 sts.

Round 5: Knit.

Rounds 6, 8, & 10: K1, M1L, K13, K2tog, SSK, K13, M1R, K1.

Rounds 7, 9, & 11: Knit.

Round 12: *SSK, K12, K2tog, repeat from * to end of round—28 sts.

Round 13: Knit.

Round 14: *SSK, K10, K2tog, repeat from * to end of round—24 sts.

Round 15: Knit.

Round 16: *SSK, K8, K2tog, repeat from * to end of round—20 sts.

Round 17: Knit.

Round 18: *SSK, K6, K2tog, repeat from * to end of round—16 sts.

Round 19: Knit.

Round 20: *SSK, K4, K2tog, repeat from * to end of round—12 sts.

Round 21: Knit.

Round 22: *SSK, K2, K2tog, repeat from * to end of round—8 sts.

Round 23: Knit.

Round 24: *SSK, K2tog, repeat from * to end of round—4 sts.

Cut yarn, thread through remaining 4 sts, and pull tight.

Work opposite back flipper analogously by picking up 24 sts on the opposite side of the body and working rounds as above.

Horns

Using MC yarn, pick up 3 sts on the side of the head. See **Figure 4** for guidance in the placement of these sts.

Figure 4

Join these sts into a round and work 4 rows. Cut yarn, thread through the 3 sts and pull. Using a tapestry needle, thread this yarn end through the tip of the horn to create a blunt end.

Work the opposite horn similarly by picking up another 3 sts on the opposite side of the head.

Finishing

Using EC yarn, embroider eyes. Using a length of yarn in MC, st (mattress st) the two opposite selvedges of the tail region together. While doing this, stuff the remaining length of the tail with fiberfill, as necessary. Take care of any loose yarn ends.

Jackalope

The legend of the jackalope (also referred to as the antelabbit or stagbunny) may have originated from sightings of desert hares afflicted by a papillomavirus that caused them to sprout horny protrusions all over their bodies. The strange eyewitness accounts of these horned hares combined with the sleek athletic prowess of the desert jackrabbit likely gave rise to this comical American myth. This knit version is a challenging project, but it is well worth the effort. The body and head are worked in one piece, with openings for hind legs incorporated into the sides of the flank. Then, the hind legs are knitted onto these designated openings, and the front legs are attached to the underside. Antlers, ears, and tail are all worked separately and sewn on.

yarn

Worsted weight
MC (lichen heather): 200 yd (183 m)
Shown: Cascade 220 Heathers color #7806
CC1 (cerulean): 25 yd (23 m)
Shown: Cascade 220 color #8908
CC2 (natural white): 25 yd (23 m)
Shown: Cascade 220 color #8010

needles

- Two sets U.S. size 5 (3.75 mm) double-pointed needles
and/or
- Two U.S. size 5 (3.75 mm) circular needles, 24" (61 cm) long
- Two stitch holders

notions

- Fiberfill stuffing
- Tapestry needle
- Four 12" (30.5 cm) chenille stems (optional)

gauge

22 to 24 sts = 4" (10 cm) in stockinette stitch

dimensions

Body length: 12" (30.5 cm)

difficulty

Experienced

Pattern

Head and Body

In MC, CO 20 sts. Continue, working back and forth in rows, as follows:

Row 1: Sl1, P17, w&t.

Row 2: K3, [M1R, K2, M1L, K2] 3 times, K1, w&t—26 sts.

Row 3: P20, w&t.

Row 4: K2, M1R, K2, M1L, K4, M1R, K2, M1L, K4, M1R, K2, M1L, K2, w&t—32 sts.

Row 5: P22, w&t.

Row 6: K1, M1R, K2, M1L, K6, M1R, K2, M1L, K6, M1R, K2, M1L, K1, w&t—38 sts.

Row 7: P24, w&t.

Row 8: K2, M1L, K8, M1R, K2, M1L, K8, M1R, K2, w&t—42 sts.

Row 9: P22, w&t.

Row 10: K8, M1R, K2, M1L, K8, w&t—44 sts.

Row 11: P16, w&t.

Row 12: K5, M1R, K2, M1L, K5, w&t—46 sts.

Row 13: P16, w&t.

Row 14: K8, M1R, K2, M1L, K8, w&t—48 sts.

Row 15: P24, w&t.

Row 16: K13, M1R, K2, M1L, K13, w&t—50 sts.

Row 17: P33, w&t.

Row 18: K17, M1R, K2, M1L, K17, w&t—52 sts.

Row 19: P40, w&t.

Row 20: K20, M1R, K2, M1L, K20, w&t—54 sts.

Row 21: P46, w&t.

Row 22: K48, w&t.

Row 23: P50, K1.

Row 24: Sl1, K53.

Row 25: Sl1, P49, w&t.

Row 26: K46, w&t.

Row 27: P42, w&t.

Row 28: K38, w&t.

Row 29: P34, w&t.

Row 30: K30, w&t.

Row 31: P26, w&t.

Row 32: K22, w&t.

Row 33: P37, K1.

Row 34: Sl1, K53.

To create openings for placement of the hind legs, BO and CO sts on the next two rows as follows:

Row 35: Sl1, P2; P17, transferring these 17 sts onto a st holder or cable; P14; P17, transferring these 17 sts onto a second st holder or cable; P2, K1—20 sts.

Row 36: Sl1, K2; turn work, and, using the cable CO method, CO 14 sts; turn work; K14; turn work, and, using the cable CO method, CO 14 sts; turn work; K3—48 sts.

Continue, working back and forth in rows, as follows:

Row 37: Sl1, P46, K1.

Row 38: Sl1, K47.

Row 39: Sl1, P43, w&t.

Row 40: K40, w&t.

Row 41: P36, w&t.

Row 42: K32, w&t.

Row 43: P28, w&t.

Row 44: K24, w&t.

Row 45: P20, w&t.

Row 46: K16, w&t.

Row 47: P31, K1.

Row 48: Sl1, K47.

Rows 49–58: Repeat rows 39–48.

Row 59: Sl1, P46, K1.

Row 60: Sl1, SSK, K42, K2tog, K1—46 sts.

Rows 61 & 63: Sl1, P44, K1.

Row 62: Sl1, K45.

Row 64: Sl1, SSK, K40, K2tog, K1—44 sts.

Rows 65 & 67: Sl1, P42, K1.

Row 66: Sl1, K43.

Row 68: Sl1, SSK, K38, K2tog, K1—42 sts.

Rows 69 & 71: Sl1, P40, K1.

Row 70: Sl1, K41.

Row 72: Sl1, SSK, K36, K2tog, K1—40 sts.

Row 73: Sl1, P2, w&t.

Row 74: K3.

Row 75: Sl1, P4, w&t.

Row 76: K2, K2tog, K1—39 sts.

Row 77: Sl1, P5, w&t.

Row 78: K6.

Row 79: Sl1, P7, w&t.

Row 80: K5, K2tog, K1—38 sts.

Row 81: Sl1, P8, w&t.

Row 82: K9.

Row 83: Sl1, P10, w&t.

Row 84: K8, K2tog, K1—37 sts.

Row 85: Sl1, P35, K1.

Row 86: Sl1, K2, w&t.

Row 87: P2, K1.

Row 88: Sl1, SSK, K2, w&t—36 sts.

Row 89: P3, K1.

Row 90: Sl1, K5, w&t.

Row 91: P5, K1.

Row 92: Sl1, SSK, K5, w&t—35 sts.

Row 93: P6, K1.

Row 94: Sl1, K8, w&t.

Row 95: P8, K1.

Row 96: Sl1, SSK, K8, w&t—34 sts.

Row 97: P9, K1.

Row 98: Sl1, K33.

Row 99: Sl1, P3, w&t.

Row 100: K4.

Row 101: Sl1, P6, w&t.

Row 102: K7.

Row 103: Sl1, P9, w&t.

Row 104: K10.

Row 105: Sl1, P12, w&t.

Row 106: K13.

Row 107: Sl1, P32, K1.

Row 108: Sl1, K3, w&t.

Row 109: P3, K1.

Row 110: Sl1, K6, w&t.

Row 111: P6, K1.

Row 112: Sl1, K9, w&t.

Row 113: P9, K1.

Row 114: Sl1, K12, w&t.

Row 115: P12, K1.

Row 116: Sl1, SSK, K28, K2tog, K1—32 sts.

Row 117: Sl1, P30, K1.

Row 118: Sl1, SSK, K26, K2tog, K1—30 sts.

Row 119: Sl1, P28, K1.

Row 120: Sl1, SSK, K24, K2tog, K1—28 sts.

Row 121: Sl1, P25, w&t.

Row 122: K24, w&t.

Row 123: P22, w&t.

Row 124: K8, M1R, K4, M1L, K8, w&t—30 sts.

Row 125: P20, w&t.

Row 126: K7, M1R, K4, M1L, K7, w&t—32 sts.

Row 127: P18, w&t.

Row 128: K6, M1R, K4, M1L, K6, w&t—34 sts.

Row 129: P19, w&t.

Row 130: K8, M1R, K4, M1L, K8, w&t—36 sts.

Row 131: P24, w&t.

Row 132: K26, w&t.

Row 133: P28, w&t.

Row 134: K30, w&t.

Row 135: P32, K1.

Row 136: Sl1, K35.

Turn work. Use the cable CO method to CO 2 sts. Turn work again and join these 38 sts into a round. Continue:

Round 1: K37, place marker to designate the beginning of all subsequent rounds.

Round 2: K3, M1L, K32, M1R, K3—40 sts.

Round 3: Knit.

Round 4: K11, SSK, K14, K2tog, K11—38 sts.

Round 5: Knit.

Round 6: K11, SSK, K12, K2tog, K11—36 sts.

Round 7: K11, SSK, K10, K2tog, K11—34 sts.

Round 8: K11, SSK, K8, K2tog, K11—32 sts.

Round 9: K11, SSK, K6, K2tog, K11—30 sts.

Round 10: SSK, K9, SSK, K4, K2tog, K9, K2tog—26 sts.

Round 11: K10, SSK, K2, K2tog, K10—24 sts.

Round 12: SSK, K8, SSK, K2tog, K8, K2tog—20 sts.

Round 13: SSK, K16, K2tog—18 sts.

Round 14: SSK, K14, K2tog—16 sts.

Round 15: SSK, K12, K2tog—14 sts.

Round 16: SSK 2 times, K6, K2tog 2 times—10 sts.

Round 17: SSK, K6, K2tog—8 sts.

Cut yarn, thread through final 8 sts, and pull tight.

Hind Legs

To work the right hind leg, use MC to knit the right-most 17 sts held on the st holder on one side of the left hind leg opening. Pick up 1 additional st at the highest point of the opening. Turn work. Using a new needle, pick up another 18 sts from the CO edge on the opposite side of the leg opening. You should now have a total of 36 sts spanning the left hind leg opening. Use **Figure 1** as a guide.

Figure 1

Continue, working back and forth in rows:

Row 1: Sl1, P31, w&t.

Row 2: K12, M1R, K4, M1L, K12, w&t—38 sts.

Row 3: P26, w&t.

Row 4: K9, M1R, K4, M1L, K9, w&t—40 sts.

Row 5: P20, w&t.

Row 6: K16, w&t.

Row 7: P12, w&t.

Row 8: K8, w&t.

Row 9: P9, w&t.

Row 10: K10, w&t.

Row 11: P11, w&t.

Row 12: K12, w&t.

Row 13: P13, w&t.

Row 14: K4, K2tog, K2, SSK, K4, w&t—38 sts.

Row 15: P14, w&t.

Row 16: K5, K2tog, K2, SSK, K5, w&t—36 sts.

Row 17: P15, w&t.

Row 18: K5, K2tog, K2, SSK, K5, w&t—34 sts.

Row 19: P15, w&t.

Row 20: K5, K2tog, K2, SSK, K5, w&t—32 sts.

Row 21: P16, w&t.

Row 22: K6, K2tog, K2, SSK, K6, w&t—30 sts.

Row 23: P17, w&t.

Row 24: K6, K2tog, K2, SSK, K6, w&t—28 sts.

Row 25: P17, w&t.

Row 26: K6, K2tog, K2, SSK, K6, w&t—26 sts.

Row 27: P18, w&t.

Row 28: K7, K2tog, K2, SSK, K7, w&t—24 sts.

Row 29: P19, w&t.

Row 30: K7, K2tog, K2, SSK, K7, w&t—22 sts.

Row 31: P16, w&t.

Row 32: K4, K2tog, K2, SSK, K4, w&t—20 sts.

Row 33: P10, w&t.

Row 34: K1, K2tog, K2, SSK, K1, w&t—18 sts.

Row 35: P7, w&t.

Row 36: K1, K2tog, K2, SSK, K1, w&t—16 sts.

Row 37: P8, w&t.

Row 38: K2, K2tog, K2, SSK, K2, w&t—14 sts.

Row 39: P10, K1.

Row 40: Sl1, K13.

Join these 14 sts into a round and continue:

Round 1: K1, M1L, K3, K2tog, K2, SSK, K3, M1R, K1.

Round 2: Knit.

Rounds 3-6: Repeat rounds 1 & 2 two more times.

Round 7: K1, M1L, K3, K2tog, K2, SSK, K3, M1R, K1.

Round 8: K5, w&t.

Continue shaping the back of the heel by working in rows:

Row 1: P10, w&t.

Row 2: K8, w&t.

Row 3: P6, w&t.

Row 4: K4, w&t.

Row 5: P2, w&t.

Row 6: K3, w&t.

Row 7: P4, w&t.

Row 8: K2tog, SSK, K2, w&t—12 sts.

Row 9: P6, w&t.

Row 10: K1, K2tog, SSK, K3, w&t—10 sts.

Row 11: P8, w&t.

Row 12: K9.

Connect the two sides of the heel to create the top of the foot as follows: continue with MC yarn and K5; turn work. This will now serve as the beginning of your row. The remainder of the foot is worked in rows as follows:

Row 13: Sl1, P8, K1.

Row 14: Sl1, K9.

Rows 15-28: Repeat rows 13 & 14 seven more times.

Row 29: Sl1, P7, w&t.

Row 30: K2, M1R, K2, M1L, K2, w&t—12 sts.

Row 31: P6, w&t.

Row 32: K1, M1R, K2, M1L, K1, w&t—14 sts.

Row 33: P5, w&t.

Row 34: K1, M1R, K2, M1L, K1, w&t—16 sts.

Row 35: P8, w&t.

Row 36: K10, w&t.

Row 37: P12, K1.

Row 38: Sl1, K15.

BO all sts.

To work the back of the ankle, use MC to pick up 16 sts along one selvedge of the opening on the underside of the leg. Turn the work and, continuing with the same MC yarn, pick up another 16 sts on the opposite selvedge. Use **Figure 2** as a guide for picking up these sts. Cut yarn, leaving a long tail. Using a tapestry needle and this long yarn tail, graft (Kitchener stitch) the sts from the first needle to the sts from the second needle. While grafting, stuff the leg with fiberfill. If you desire a pose-able leg, fold a chenille stem in half, twist the halves together, and insert it into the hind limb while you are stuffing.

Figure 2

To work the footpad, use CC to pick up 18 sts around the circumference of the paw pad, using **Figure 3** as a guide. When picking up these sts, be sure to begin and end at the base of the footpad.

Figure 3

Join these 18 sts into a round and continue:

Round 1: Knit.

Round 2: [SSK, K5, K2tog] 2 times—14 sts.

Cut yarn, leaving a long tail. Divide sts evenly onto two needles. Using tapestry needle and this long yarn tail, graft (Kitchener stitch) the sts on the first needle to the stitches on the second needle. While grafting, stuff the paw with fiberfill. To work the left hind leg, begin at the base of the opening for the leg and pick up 18 sts along the CO edge. Turn the work, pick up 1 more st at the highest point of the opening, and knit the 17 sts remaining on the st holder. You should now have a total of 36 stitches spanning the left hind leg opening. Continue as for the right hind leg.

Front Legs *(Make 2)*

In MC, CO 4 sts. Continue, working back and forth in rows, as follows:

Row 1: Sl1, P2, K1.

Row 2: Sl1, K1, KLL, KRL, K2—6 sts.

Row 3: Sl1, P4, K1.

Row 4: Sl1, K1, M1L, K2, M1R, K2—8 sts.

Row 5: Sl1, P6, K1.

Row 6: Sl1, K1, M1L, K4, M1R, K2—10 sts.

Row 7: Sl1, P8, K1.

Row 8: Sl1, K1, M1L, K6, M1R, K2—12 sts.

Row 9: Sl1, P10, K1.

Row 10: Sl1, K1, M1L, K8, M1R, K2—14 sts.

Row 11: Sl1, P12, K1.

Row 12: Sl1, K13.

Join these 14 sts into a round and continue:

Rounds 1-3: Knit.

Round 4: K5, w&t.

Turn the heel of the foot by working in short rows as follows:

Row 1: P10, w&t.

Row 2: K8, w&t.

Row 3: P6, w&t.

Row 4: K4, w&t.

Row 5: P2, w&t.

Row 6: K3, w&t.

Row 7: P4, w&t.

Row 8: K2tog, SSK, K2, w&t—12 sts.

Row 9: P6, w&t.

Row 10: K1, K2tog, SSK, K3, w&t—10 sts.

Row 11: P8, w&t.

Row 12: K10.

Connect the two sides of the heel to create the top of the foot as follows: continue with MC yarn and K5; turn work. This will now serve as the beginning of your row. The remainder of the foot is worked in rows as follows:

Row 13: Sl1, P8, K1.

Row 14: K1, K9.

Rows 15-36: Repeat rows 13 & 14 ten more times.

Row 37: Sl1, P7, w&t.

Row 38: K2, M1R, K2, M1L, K2, w&t—12 sts.

Row 39: P6, w&t.

Row 40: K1, M1R, K2, M1L, K1, w&t—14 sts.

Row 41: P7, w&t.

Row 42: K8, w&t.

Row 43: P10, K1.

Row 44: Sl1, SSK, K8, K2tog, K1—12 sts.

Loosely BO all stitches.

Work the back of the ankle as follows. Use MC yarn to pick up 19 sts from one selvedge of the leg, beginning at the upper end of the opening and continuing toward the paw. Turn the work and, continuing with MC yarn, pick up another 19 sts from the opposite selvedge. See **Figure 4** for guidance.

Figure 4

Cut yarn, leaving a long tail. Using a tapestry needle, graft (Kitchener st) the sts from the first selvedge to the sts from the second selvedge. While grafting, stuff the leg with fiberfill. Do not overstuff. If you desire a pose-able leg, place a folded chenille stem (blunt end first) into the leg and foot.

To work the underside of the footpad, use CC to pick up 14 sts around the circumference of the paw opening. Be sure to begin at the base of the paw and continue around. Use **Figure 5** for guidance in picking up these sts. Join these sts into a round and continue:

Figure 5

Round 1: Knit.

Round 2: [SSK, K3, K2tog] 2 times—10 sts.

Cut yarn, leaving a long tail. Divide remaining stitches evenly onto two needles. Using a tapestry needle, graft (Kitchener st) the sts on the first needle to the sts on the second needle. While grafting, lightly stuff the paw with polyfill.

Underside

Use **Figure 6** as a guide for attaching the front legs to the underside of the chest. To do this, use mattress st to attach one selvedge of each leg to the adjacent selvedge on the underside of the chest.

Figure 6

Use **Figure 7** as a guide to pick up sts from the underside opening as follows: 17 sts from the left selvedge of the neck, 10 sts from selvedge of the left front leg, 20 sts from the remaining left selvedge, 18 sts from the CO edge, and 20 sts from the right selvedge moving toward the right front leg.

Figure 7

Turn work and continue:

Row 1: P58, w&t.

Row 2: K23, K2tog 5 times, K23.

Continuing with same yarn, proceed along selvedge of right front leg to pick up 10 sts, and along remaining right selvedge underneath neck to pick up another 17 sts. See **Figure 8** for guidance in picking up these sts. You should now have a grand total of 107 sts.

Figure 8

Cut yarn, leaving a long tail. Divide sts onto two needles. Using a tapestry needle and this yarn tail, graft (Kitchener st) the sts from the first needle to the sts on the second needle. While grafting, stuff the head and body of your creature. If you have used chenille stems in the front and hind legs, be sure to twist the sharp ends around each other and wrap with waste yarn.

Tail

In MC, CO 18 sts. Continue, working in rows as follows:

Row 1: Sl1, P15, w&t.

Row 2: K14, w&t.

Row 3: P12, w&t.

Row 4: K10, w&t.

Row 5: P8, w&t.

Row 6: K6, w&t.

Row 7: P5, w&t.

Row 8: K4, w&t.

Row 9: P6, w&t.

Row 10: K8, w&t.

Row 11: P10, w&t.

Row 12: K12, w&t.

Row 13: P14, K1.

Row 14: Sl1, K17.

Now, join these 18 sts into a round and continue:

Rounds 1–4: Knit.

Round 5: [SSK, K5, K2tog] 2 times—14 sts.

Round 6: Knit.

Round 7: [SSK, K3, K2tog] 2 times—10 sts.

Round 8: [SSK, K1, K2tog] 2 times—6 sts.

Round 9: Sl2-K1-P2SSO 2 times—2 sts.

Cut yarn, thread through final 2 sts, and pull tight. Stuff tail with polyfill.

Ears (Make 2)

Work the back surface of the ear as follows. In MC, CO 25 sts. Continue working in rows as follows:

Row 1: Sl1, P20, w&t.

Row 2: K19, w&t.

Row 3: P15, w&t.

Row 4: K13, w&t.

Row 5: P9, w&t.

Row 6: K12, P1.

Row 7: Sl1, P10, w&t.

Row 8: K10, P1.

Row 9: Sl1, P14, w&t.

Row 10: K14, P1.

Row 11: Sl1, P18, w&t.

Row 12: K15, w&t.

Row 13: P19, w&t.

Row 14: K21, w&t.

Row 15: P22, K1.

BO all stitches.

Work the inside of the ear as follows. In CC1, CO 6 sts. Continue, working back and forth in rows:

Row 1 & 3: Sl1, P5.

Row 2: Sl1, K4, P1.

Row 4: Sl1, K1, M1R, K2, M1L, K1, P1—8 sts.

Rows 5 & 7: Sl1, P7.

Row 6: Sl1, K6, P1.

Row 8: Sl1, K2, M1R, K2, M1L, K2, P1—10 sts.

Rows 9, 11, 13, 15, 17: Sl1, P9.

Rows 10, 12, 14, 16: Sl1, K8, P1.

Row 18: Sl1, K2, K2tog, SSK, K2, P1—8 sts.

Rows 19, 21, 23: Sl1, P7.

Rows 20 & 22: Sl1, K6, P1.

Row 24: Sl1, K1, K2tog, SSK, K1, P1—6 sts.

Rows 25, 27, 29: Sl1, P5.

Rows 26 & 28: Sl1, K4, P1.

Row 30: Sl1, K2tog, SSK, P1—4 sts.

Row 31: Sl1, P3.

Row 32: K2tog, SSK—2 sts.

Cut yarn, thread through remaining 2 sts, and pull tight.

To attach the inside portion of the ear (worked in CC1) to the back portion of the ear (worked in MC), begin by using MC to pick up 24 sts along the CO edge of the backing. Turn the work, and pick up an additional 24 sts along the BO edge of the backing. Now, continuing with MC yarn, pick up 24 sts from one selvedge of the inside portion of the ear. When picking up these sts, begin at the base of the inside portion and continue toward the tip. Be sure to pick up these sts kwise from the purl side of the work. Turn the work and pick up an additional 24 sts from the second selvedge of the inside portion.

Use **Figure 9** for guidance in picking up these sts.

Figure 9

Align the outer portion of the ear with the inner portion of the ear. Continuing with MC yarn, use the three-needle BO method to BO all sts and attach the outside and inside aspects of the ear together.

Antlers *(Make 2)*

Work the base segment of the antler as follows. Use CC2 yarn to CO 5 sts. Work as I-cord:

Rows 1–9: Knit.

Row 10: K2, K2tog, K1—4 sts.

Rows 11–13: Knit.

Row 14: K1, K2tog, K1—3 sts.

Rows 15–17: Knit.

Row 18: K2tog, K1—2 sts.

Cut yarn, thread through remaining 2 sts, and pull tight. Thread yarn tail through second st one more time to create a pointed tip.

Now, work the first branching segment of the antler as follows. Use CC2 to pick up 2 sts approximately 1.25" (3 cm) from the base of the antler. Turn the work, and pick up another 2 sts directly behind the first 2 sts. Work these 4 sts as I-cord as follows:

Rows 1–4: Knit.

Row 5: K1, K2tog, K1—3 sts.

Rows 6–8: Knit.

Row 9: K2tog, K1—2 sts.

Cut yarn, thread through remaining 2 sts, and pull tight. As for first segment of antler, thread yarn tail through second st one more time to create a pointed tip.

Work the second (and final) branching segment of the antler by picking up 2 sts on the first branching segment, approximately 0.75" (2 cm) from where it intersects with the antler base. Turn the work, and pick up another st directly behind these first 2 sts, for a total of 3 sts. Work these sts as I-cord as follows:

Rows 1–6: Knit.

Row 7: K2tog, K1—2 sts.

Cut yarn, thread through final 2 sts, and pull tight. As for the first two segments of the antler, thread the yarn through the second st one more time to create a pointed tip.

Finishing

Attach the two ears and two antlers to the top of the head. Use photographs of models as a guide to placement of these structures. Attach the tail to the rear of the body. Use dark brown yarn to embroider the eyes and nose. Take care of any loose yarn ends.

Knitting Abbreviations

Beg	begin		**P1-f&b**	purl into front and back loop of same stitch
Bet	between		**P2tog**	purl two stitches together
BO	bind off		**PSSO**	pass slipped stitch(es) over
CC	contrasting color		**Patt**	pattern
cm	centimeters		**pwise**	purlwise
CO	cast on		**Rep**	repeat
Cont	continue		**Rev St stitch**	reverse Stockinette stitch
Dec	decrease		**Rnd(s)**	rounds
Dpn(s)	double-pointed needle(s)		**RS**	right side
g	grams		**Sk**	skip
Inc	increase		**Sl**	slip
K	knit		**Sl st**	slip stitch
Kl-f&b	knit into front and back loop of same stitch		**SSK**	slip, slip, knit decrease
K2tog	knit two stitches together		**st(s)**	stitch(es)
KRL	right loop increase		**St st**	Stockinette stitch
KLL	left loop increase		**tbl**	through back loop
kwise	knitwise		**WS**	wrong side
m(s)	markers(s)		**wyb**	with yarn in back
MC	main color		**wyf**	with yarn in front
rem	remaining or remain		**w&t**	wrap and turn
mm	millimeters		**YO**	yarn over needle
M1	make one stitch (increase)		*****	repeat from *
M1R	make one right		**[ ]**	repeat instructions in brackets as directed
M1L	make one left		**—**	number of stitches that should be on the needle or across a row
P	purl			

About the Author

Hansi Singh began designing knit amigurumi creatures as playmates for her infant son. Hansigurumi, a shop she opened on Etsy for selling her amigurumi patterns, caught the attention (and needles!) of knitters in the US and abroad, and became an overnight success. Hailed "an amazing up and coming crafter" by CRAFT magazine, she lives in Seattle with her partner Aaron and son Ambrose.

Acknowledgments

My partner Aaron Barker has my eternal gratitude for putting up with the demon in me through the process of designing the critters in this book. A special thanks to the following amazing individuals for their support and encouragement: Sarah Lanzillota, Kristen Rask, Moxie, Chris Crites, and Lena Kai. Thanks to my editor, Linda Neubauer, for giving me the opportunity to write this book, and to write it well, and to Sylvia McArdle for the wonderful art direction. Finally, a special shout-out to Cascade Yarns for donating the beautiful fiber used for the projects in this book.

Index

Dedication

For my partner Aaron and my son Ambrose, who have taught me
to embrace the world and its many peculiarities.